THE SEXUAL MOUNTAIN
AND BLACK WOMEN WRITERS

The Sexual Mountain and Black Women Writers

ADVENTURES IN SEX, LITERATURE, AND REAL LIFE

Calvin C. Hernton

ANCHOR PRESS
Doubleday
NEW YORK
1987

This hardcover edition is the first publication of *The Sexual Mountain and Black Women Writers*.

Anchor Press edition: 1987

Versions of the following material have appeared in the respective publications:

Chapter 2: "The Sexual Mountain and Black Women Writers" in *Black American Literature Forum*, v. 18, n. 4, Winter 1984, also in the *Black Scholar*, v. 16, n. 4, July/August 1985.

Chapter 4: "Black Women in the Life and Work of Langston Hughes" in *Survival and Renewal* (World Fellowship) 1980.

Chapter 5: "Black Women Poets: The Oral Narrative Tradition" published as "The Tradition" in *Parnassus*, v. 12, n. 2/v.13, n. 1, Spring/Summer, Fall/Winter 1985.

Library of Congress Cataloging-in-Publication Data

Hernton, Calvin C.
The sexual mountain and Black women writers.

Bibliography: p. 042219
Includes index. 16,95
1. American literature—Afro-American authors—
History and criticism. 2. American literature—
Women authors—History and criticism. 3. American
literature—20th century—History and criticism.
4. Afro-American women in literature. 5. Women
and literature—United States. 6. Feminism and
literature—United States. 7. Sex in literature.
8. Afro-Americans in literature. 9. Sex role in
literature. I. Title.
PS153.N5H47 1987 810'.9'9287 87-467

ISBN: 0-385-23921-1

ACKNOWLEDGMENTS

Grateful acknowledgment is made for permission to reprint the following:

"And Still I Rise" by Maya Angelou, copyright © 1978 by Maya Angelou. Reprinted by permission.

Excerpts from *Selected Poems of Langston Hughes* by Langston Hughes, copyright © 1959 by Langston Hughes. Reprinted by permission. "my blues ain't pretty" from *The Sweet Flypaper of Life* by Langston Hughes and Roy Decarava, copyright © 1955 by Langston Hughes and Roy Decarava.

Excerpts from *Natural Birth* by Toi Derricotte, copyright © 1983 by Toi Derricotte. Reprinted by permission. "Hester's Song" by Toi Derricotte from *Home Girls*, copyright © 1983 by Toi Derricotte. Reprinted by permission.

Excerpts from *Ceremony for Minneconjoux* by Brenda Marie Osbey, copyright © 1983 by Brenda Marie Osbey. Reprinted by permission.

Excerpts from *Playing the Changes* by Thulani Davis, copyright © 1985 by Thulani Davis. Reprinted by permission.

Excerpts from *Queen of the Ebony Isles* by Colleen J. McElroy, copyright © 1984 by Colleen J. McElroy. Reprinted by permission.

Excerpts from *Narratives: Poems in the Traditions of Black Women* by Cheryl Clarke, copyright © 1983 by Cheryl Clarke.

Excerpts from *Museum* by Rita Dove, copyright © 1983 by Rita Dove. Reprinted by permission.

"The Black Goddess" by Donna Kate Rushin, copyright © 1983 by Donna Kate Rushin. Reprinted by permission.

DEDICATED
TO
THE MEMORY OF SARAH WEBSTER FABIO
JUJU IN HER RAINBOW

I wish to express my thanks to the many students in my literature classes at Oberlin College. I specifically express my gratitude and indebtedness to Adriene Cannon, Jacqueline Barrien, Sarah Norton, Michele Welsing, and Alice Passer.

Mary Gilfus has contributed to this work in more ways than I can name. I am eternally grateful for her technical and critical assistance, her encouragement and endurance.

I have benefited valuably from the critical, resourceful energies of the poet Regina Williams.

Contents

Should you, my lord, while you peruse my Song
Wonder from whence my love of *Freedom* sprung,
Whence flow these wishes for the common good,
By feeling hearts alone best understood,
I, young in life, by seeming cruel fate
Was snatch'd from *Afri's* fancy'd happy feet:
What pangs excruciating must molest,
What sorrows labour in my parent's breast?
Steel'd was that foul and by no misery mov'd
That from a father seiz'd his babe belov'd:
Such, such my case. And can I then but pray
Others may never feel tyrannic sway?

                         —PHILLIS WHEATLEY, 1772

You may write me down in history
With your bitter, twisted lies,
You may trod me in the very dirt
But still, like dust, I'll rise.

You may shoot me with your words,
You may cut me with your eyes,
You may kill me with your hatefulness,
But still, like air, I'll rise.

Leaving behind nights of terror and fear
I rise
Into a daybreak that's wondrously clear
I rise
Bringing the gifts that my ancestors gave,

I rise
I rise
I rise.

—MAYA ANGELOU, from *Still I Rise*, 1978

I know that it feels a kind o' hissin' and ticklin' like to see a colored woman get up and tell you about things, and Woman's Right. We have all been thrown down so low that nobody thought we'd ever get up again; but we have been long enough trodden now; we will come up again. . . . You may hiss as much as you like, but it is comin'. Women don't get half as much rights as they ought to; we want more, and we will have it . . . I'm round watchin' these things . . . I'm sittin' among you to watch; and every once and awhile I will come out and tell you what time of night it is.

—SOJOURNER TRUTH, 1853

Introduction

This book presents and examines the facts and fantasies surrounding black women writers. In writings by black women and a sample of "feministic" writing by a black man, the book focuses on crucial issues in sex, politics, literature, and real life.

In October of 1985, a meeting convened in Brooklyn, New York, for the purpose of founding a black publishing communications enterprise that would publish a black daily newspaper, books, magazines, journals, and other media. Money would be no obstacle, since, it was said, backers were already secured. Although a few women were there, the meeting was chaired by a man, and black males dominated the gathering. The clincher came when the speaker explained the motivation behind the launching of the proposed enterprise. He went into a tirade against black women writers, calling them out of their names and claiming they had "taken over" the publishing world in a "conspiracy" against black men writers. He alleged that the women were using their pens to "put down" black men before the eyes of the world. The most accusative of such remarks were hurled at Toni Morrison and Alice Walker, the latter of whom was specifically charged with being an "avowed lesbian."

The present book fulfills the burning need for a black male writer to speak out against the red bricks of slander and bigotry that are hurled at black women and the literature they produce. The first black writer in America to achieve worldwide recognition was Phillis Wheatley, a black woman. But because men have historically dominated the world of black literature and black thought, the annals that chart the stages of black writing have been written exclusively by men, wherein they have glorified their own writings to the exclusion of the women's. Black women writers have been treated as "literary domestics," serving as cooks, baby-sitters, stamp-lickers, girlfriends, wives, and "sexual sport" for the men.

This book examines the controversial role that black women

have played and are playing in the making of Black American Literature. It is a positive appraisal of the much maligned writings of today's black women. It documents the sexist bigotry of black males and confirms that black women authors are celebrating a literary Fourth of July for the first time in America.

The overriding purpose of this book then is to promote understanding of the literature written by both black women and men. It shows how to read black women writings of all persuasions. It seeks to "clear the air" about the sexual politics between black women and black men writers. It endeavors to show where the women are coming from, the tradition and heritage of yesterday's and today's black women writers from Phillis Wheatley to Maya Angelou, from "Should You Wonder" to "Still I Rise."

The book attempts to step beyond the murky controversy of today's black women writers and chart a clear path for the future.

C.C.H.

THE SEXUAL MOUNTAIN
AND BLACK WOMEN WRITERS

ONE

Who's Afraid of Alice Walker?

THE COLOR PURPLE AS SLAVE NARRATIVE

In the middle of the 1980s, black men and women were entangled in hot controversy over the all-black Hollywood film "The Color Purple." Millions of people went to see it. But none of them seemed to know what they were looking at. Nobody recognized that "The Color Purple" was, and is, a slave narrative.

A slave narrative is the autobiography of a slave. More accurately, a slave narrative is the life-story of a former slave who has somehow gained freedom, usually through many trials and hardships. Slaves, of course, were not permitted to read and write. They were severely punished and even killed if they were caught trying to learn to read. Therefore, many former slaves had to tell—"narrate"—their life-stories to a person who could write. Usually the person lived in the North, and wrote down the stories in keeping with the story-telling styles of the former slaves. More often, though, the narratives were written by former slaves themselves who had secretly acquired literacy during slavery. They had been clandestinely taught by a privileged literate Negro or a kind white person, or the former slaves themselves had learned to write in the North after having somehow gained freedom.

Slave narratives first appeared in rudimentary form during the latter part of the 1700s. They reached full development between 1830 and 1865, during which time they became a unique and special genre of black literature and were the most controversial, most popular form of writing in America.

The narratives were not written just for the sake of creating literature or art. Nor were they written to aggrandize the egos of their authors. Like all black writing, the primary inspiration and the primary intent for writing slave narratives were to enlighten the world about the oppression of black people and to enlist the world in the eradication of that oppression. Specifically, the autobiographies of the slaves were purposely written as Anti-Slavery Literature. They were very instrumental in the Abolition Movement, in the cultural, political, and moral battle that led to the Civil War, which liberated the slaves.

Characteristically, slave narratives have a beginning, a middle and an end. The format involves a succession of episodes, incidents, scenes and intermittent passages of moral outcry: "Look, look, Dear Reader, see how terrible the situation is!"

The narratives take us through the daily round of plantation life, they show how the slaves work, eat, think and survive in a world of systematic enslavement. We witness cruelty, violence, and human frailty so repugnant that we find it difficult to believe or imagine. We see loved ones mercilessly torn apart and sold away. We witness rapes, beatings and killings. We see a total disregard for the family and dignity of the slaves. We experience moments of stolen joy that suddenly turn to bleak tragedy, and we witness the slaves' sweat and labor for which they are not paid and not appreciated. Alas, through constant torture and deprivation, we see human beings conditioned into believing in the superiority of their oppressors and reduced to an incredible mentality of self-loathing and personal negation. The scenes in which these incidents and episodes occur are set against the beauty and splendor of the natural environment of the southern landscape, which serves to heighten the wretchedness of human bondage.

By now we are in the middle of the life-story of the slave. A

desire for freedom has been kindled in the slave. The desire for
freedom is a rising in slave consciousness born of suffering and
surviving, and born of a unique inspirational experience, such
as a religious vision or a gradual "possession" by the will to die
or be free. Suspense mounts as the slave grows in courage and
embarks upon escape, finally to arrive in the North—where the
former slave becomes a worker, an orator, an autobiographer, a
free person enlisted in the cause to liberate the sisters and
brothers left behind in bondage.

[2]

In both form and content, this is what "The Color Purple" is.
It is an emulation of the slave narrative, which is a black-invented art form and a classical (primal) literary genre. The subject matter of "The Color Purple" is the substance out of which
all slave narratives are made—Oppression and the Process of
Liberation. This is what we see when we see the film.

The film, however, is not a slave narrative, it is not the autobiography of a known person. Rather, the film is based on a
work of fiction, a novel. But the distinction between slave narrative and fiction is an artificiality. At best, the distinction is a
technicality that has always been and still is irrelevant, even
inimical, to the development, as well as to the very origin, nature, and purpose of black narrative literature.

Historically, the slave narrative and black fiction originated
about the same time, out of the same circumstances, and developed along the same lines. The cross-fertilization between the
slave narrative and the black novel is an important part of what
goes to make up the black literary tradition. In fact, black fiction
grew out of black autobiography, and slave narratives and black
novels have often been written by the same authors. *Clotell, or
the President's Daughter,* by William Wells Brown, the first black
novel, contains the same kind of material that is found in the
slave narratives, including the narrative of Brown's own life.
The material of slave narratives, and the very atmosphere of
slave narratives, predominate in Martin Delany's 1856 novel
Blake, or the Huts of America.

Uncle Tom's Cabin, the most acclaimed novel of the nineteenth century, was nothing less than an assemblage of incidents, episodes, scenes and characters taken from personal interviews with former slaves, popularized slave incidents, and from actual slave narratives already in print. Frederick Douglass and the Reverend Josiah Henson were among the former slaves interviewed. The Reverend Henson identified himself and was publicly acknowledged as the model for Mrs. Stowe's most incredible character, Uncle Tom. Once she had collected the material, Mrs. Stowe then proceeded to imitate the form and other attributes that are characteristic of slave narratives. Variously subtitled "Life Among the Lowly" and "The Man That Was a Thing," *Uncle Tom's Cabin* was the first successful slave-narrative rip-off ("covered") by a white author.

On the other side of the coin, the autobiographies of Henry "Box" Brown, William and Ellen Craft, Frederick Douglass, and Booker T. Washington contain the substance and attributes of black fiction. The 1853 autobiography of Solomon Northup, *Twelve Years a Slave,* reads like a fictional thriller. It was made into a television movie starring Avery Brooks as Solomon Northup. The generic relationship between slave narratives and black fiction is also manifest in any number of modern black novels. There is, for example, Margaret Walker's novel *Jubilee.* Of course, there is the novel by Ernest Gains entitled *The Autobiography of Miss Jane Pittman,* which was made into a film starring Cicely Tyson.

Turning the coin back over, a resurgence of black autobiographies in modern times took place during the 1960s. *Manchild in the Promised Land* was the first one, then came Alex Haley's *The Autobiography of Malcolm X,* followed by Eldridge Cleaver's *Soul on Ice* and a series of "life-story" writings authored by inmates of prisons. *Up from the Walking Dead* by Charles McGregor and the book by the "Soledad Brother" George Jackson are good examples of the prison genre. Naturally, the modern autobiographical writings were updated, wherein the slave plantation was replaced by the oppressive conditions of the urban ghetto. Ishmael Reed refers to these writings as "Neo-Slave Narratives." Ultimately, the most modern fusion of traditional narrative and fictional elements, along with contemporary research methods, is Haley's *Roots,* which is a blockbusting slave-narrative thriller.

Slave narratives read like fiction and fiction reads like slave narratives. This is true in terms of format, structure, and substance. It is equally true of intent and purpose. Slave narratives and black fiction focus on key individuals. The authors of autobiographies and the heroes of novels are one and the same, they are protagonists, they become prototypes of their situations. But the autobiographies and the novels also deal with the collective situation of the group with whom the key individuals share a common oppression. Moreover, the autobiographies and novels portray the process of overcoming that oppression, both in concrete terms and in terms of the self-negating emotions of the protagonists.

This is where The Color Purple is coming from. This is the tradition that informs both the novel and the film.* But with one all-important difference.

[3]

Historically, black narrative literature has been devoted to portraying whites oppressing blacks and the blacks surviving and struggling to overcome that oppression. The Color Purple, the book and the movie, breaks this tradition, or rather, it *advances* the tradition. Instead of white-on-black oppression, the primary subject matter of The Color Purple is black-on-black oppression.

Specifically, The Color Purple portrays black men as oppressors and brutalizers of black women. This means, in this instance, that a black woman took possession of a black-invented literary form that black men have always dominated and have always assumed as being exclusively their own property. If black

* Because I feel that the film sufficiently captures the substance and intentionality of the novel, most of my discussion refers to both the novel and the film in the same breath without distinguishing between them, and I collectively refer to them by capitalizing the first letters in the title without italics or quotation marks, The Color Purple. When I feel, however, that certain differences between the novel and the film warrant separate treatment, I discuss them separately by indicating the book in italics, *The Color Purple,* and by indicating the movie in quotation marks, "The Color Purple."

women were to use this powerful literary vehicle, they were supposed to use it in defense of the "whole" race—i.e., in defense of black men—to expose and decry white racism, white capitalism, and so on. Instead, Alice Walker utilizes the slave narrative to reveal the enslavement that black men level against black women.

To employ the tradition and attributes of the autobiographical narrative for this purpose is indeed a radical leap forward. It is to utilize the narrative genre in a way never fully utilized before. In fact, Walker repossessed the genre, for it belongs as much to women as to men, and she *womanized* it.

It was precisely the Womanization of the slave-narrative form that enraged so many black men—writers, intellectuals, and race leaders in particular. Walker's definition of "womanist" is instructive:

> A black feminist or feminist of color. From the black folk expression of mothers to female children. "You acting womanish," i.e., like a woman. Usually referring to outrageous, audacious, courageous or *willful* behavior. Wanting to know more and in greater depth than is considered "good" for one. . . . A woman who loves other women. . . . Appreciates and prefers women's culture, women's emotional flexibility . . . and women's strength. . . . Committed to survival and wholeness of entire people, male *and* female.

Although as many men appear in The Color Purple as do women, The Color Purple is a womanish story. In the most personal writing, letters, the story is narrated by the woman who is the protagonist, Celie. All the other sympathetic characters are women. Women squabble, women support, women love, and women heal each other. Women grow together. They become *womanish.* Men perceived this as Alice Walker's having taken a traditionally male-owned literary genre and turned it against the men. Black men could not digest this. They felt it as a damning blow to their male-supremist egos. Hence, in a very literal sense, black men were offended by the truth. They experienced feelings of betrayal, they suffered painful rage, they did what all oppressors do: Accuse and denounce. They accused the film of committing injustice against black men, they denounced

Alice Walker as a subversive for daring to make public the barbarity of black men. But what about the substance of The Color Purple and its developmental process?

[4]

The time could be anytime from the 1920s until now. The place is anywhere in the Deep or not-so Deep South. The class of blacks are southern peasantry, common salt-of-the-earth folk. They are poor, but they have shelter and they are not starving. Historically, we are aware that in the South, white racism is rampant, and that customarily rural black people are sharecroppers on land that is owned by whites who exploit and impoverish the blacks. But in Celie's world, white racism is removed until the town scenes; and on the home front, whites are simply not in the picture. The specific emphasis is on the fact that black women are brutalized by black men out of the men's own volition.

With no whites in view, an all-black world, or an all-black milieu, is seen in stark relief. It is a milieu in which the relations between women and men are characterized by subjugation and domination. The men are believers in male supremacy, which seethes in every nook and cranny of their world. From the bedroom to the kitchen to the field, the status and role of the men are superior, while the women are wantonly exploited and demeaned by the men. In short, it is an all-black milieu in which men are masters and women are slaves.

The inescapable irony of the situation is its relentless analogy to the system of slavery itself, and, later on, jim crow. Slavery and jim crow were rationalized and justified by white people's claim to racial superiority. In the name of white supremacy, every imaginable act of human atrocity was perpetrated against the blacks. Now, in an all-black situation, we witness a chillingly similar type of oppression, we see sundry acts of inhumanity leveled against black females. We are forced to realize that the centuries of slavery and racism, and the struggle to overcome them, have not informed the humanity of black men when it comes to black women. Similar to other people who have been colonized and oppressed at one time or another, the oppressive experiences of black men have not deterred them from being oppressors themselves.

The situation is indeed an ironic analogy of the highest similarity. We, for example, cannot help noticing the likeness of Albert's house and the lay of his land to the romanticized slave environment of the "Old Dominion." The glorified version of slavery was symbolized by and set in the midst of an idyllic landscape through which the Southern aristocracy visualized their cruel system in utopian terms. Just as the plantation majesty highlighted the wretchedness of the slaves, the idyllic environmental scenery of "The Color Purple" film spotlights the bitter lot of Celie and her sister Nettie. While the opening scene is one of sisterly play and carefree camaraderie, we are soon jolted out of the idyllic Camelot world of girlish delight into a scene depicting the barbarity of Celie's real life. The romantic splendor of the film's opening is abruptly contradicted by the stark revelation that Celie is "big" as a house. Alone in a dimly lit cubicle of a room, Celie gives agonizing birth as the image of a man stands menacingly in the doorway. The man rips the baby from its mother's arms and issues a warning as he vanishes into the night: "You better tell nobody but God."

This is the *germinal* scene. It contains the essence of all that Celie suffers at the hands of Mister Albert and the other men throughout the narrative. While the scene is graphically real, it is also a brilliant representational image. The male figure stands in the doorway at a distance, coldly watching the helpless girl as she suffers the birth of her child. His awesome image inhibits the light and blocks passage through the door. Light represents life, the doorway represents the womb. Then he strips the baby from its mother's grasp. The male figure is himself and is also the figure of all men. He is a menace, not just to Celie, but to all females. Having impregnated Celie and now taking her baby, he ravishes and plunders the bodies of all women. Hence, he claims ownership over the female sex, an ownership that assumes the power to exploit and deprive women of all they possess, including their sexuality.

From this scene onward, especially in the novel, Alice Walker's mastery of Celie's own voice through her letters is uniquely inventive, because the letters assume the structural format and developmental process consistent with the tradition of the black narrative genre. Through her supple use of letters, Walker depicts and portrays the details of Celie's enslavement in both its objective and subjective dimensions. Characteristic of all slave narratives, in a sequential progression of episodes, incidents and scenes that depict physical brutality, torture, trials and tribulations, economic and sexual exploitation, and the inequality and injustice of it all, Walker shows the extreme barbarity of Celie's oppression and evokes heartrending moments of pathos. Walker, moreover, shows how the enslaved Celie, under the constant weight of physical abuse, comes to have a concomitant self-negating psychology toward herself and all members of her sex group. Trapped, alienated and helpless, Celie strains to survive. In the process she accommodates herself to the status quo. Similar to all people who experience intensive deprivation and abuse, Celie internalizes the negative definition of herself that her masters hold toward and force upon her. A "slave mentality" results, fostering inarticulateness, self-depreciation, and a confused lack of identity. When Celie tells Harpo that he should beat Sophia to bring her under his thumb, and when she mumbles to Sophia that she accepts her lowly status in life because her reward is in heaven, Walker demonstrates that a slave mentality, however "compensatory," is a consequential psychological symptom of being under the concrete torture of a rigorous and persistent oppression.

In an amazingly tempered pace Alice Walker reveals, furthermore, that Celie's situation is not merely an individual "isolated incident." This is in keeping with the generic imperatives of the slave-narrative tradition. As indicated at the outset, the main purpose of slave autobiographies and black fiction is to make *public* the injustices suffered by the protagonist. Equally important is to show the connection of the protagonist's suffering with the suffering of the entire group of which the protagonist is a member, and to show that the oppression of both the protagonist and the group belongs to a world in which every member of the group suffers. It is the business of the black narrative genre to examine, expose and identify (name!) this world as a specific mode of oppression.

Accordingly, Walker shows that the individual world of Celie (and Nettie) is a collective world in which all females are considered inferior and are subject to degradation and brutality by the males. The subjugation and demeanment that Albert levels against Celie is more or less *normal* for all men, because the beliefs, feelings, ideas, attitudes and behaviors of Albert toward Celie are shared, to some degree or another, by all men toward all women. Not a single male does anything to help Celie. Hence, they support Albert's brutal oppression of Celie by their silence and by their tacit, if not blatant, support of his attitudes and actions. To wit, the social cultural *milieu* in which Celie finds herself, and all of its ideas, institutions, and practices pertaining to women and men, constitute a World of Sexism.

[5]

It has been pointed out that the world of sexism is almost an exact copy of the world of racism. In a racist world, prejudices, demeaning myths, superstitions, inequalities, and unjust and abusive practices are believed in, maintained, and leveled against all people of color by all people who are white. Black people, for example, have a lower status than whites and are assigned inferior, thankless roles, and in the presence of whites they are supposed to behave in a self-demeaning manner, like shuffling their feet and holding their heads bowed.

The same type of ideas, myths, superstitions, inequalities, and practices against people of the female sex are integral aspects of sexist environments. Just as white people have created and maintained a racist culture, so have men created and maintained a sexist culture. Racist culture teaches all whites to be racists in some manner or another. In and through an elaborate system of masculine versus feminine gender imperatives, sexist culture socializes all men to be sexists. Masculine is Master, and feminine is underling.

The ideological and behavioral inequalities fostered on blacks by whites were referred to by Richard Wright as "the ethics of living jim crow." Similarly, the familiar axioms that women's place is in the kitchen and the bedroom, that women should be seen and not heard, that women should be kept barefoot, pregnant and penniless, that they should be isolated, immobile and obedient, plus all the other ideas and beliefs underpinning the customs, conventions and practices that mandate women as inferior subjects of men—all of these things may be collectively referred to as *the ethics of living sexism.*

[6]

The ethics of living sexism was what people were witnessing when they saw "The Color Purple," or when they read the book. Both the film and the novel go beyond the stock excuse for female abuse as isolated incidents committed by misguided men who are frustrated by the economic and political injustices of American racism, which prevent them from realizing their manhood. The Color Purple thoroughly discredits this notion, better known as the "frustration-aggression-take-it-out-on-the-woman" explanation. Then, too, even so, why must women be the socially approved scapegoats for men's frustration? Two wrongs do not make a right.

On the contrary, the novel and the movie show that male brutality against women is endemic to an entire way of life that believes in the natural supremacy of men over women. Presumably, Albert is frustrated because he does not have the woman of his choice, Shug Avery, and because Celie is "ugly." But this is no excuse for his treatment of her. Or rather, that is all that it is, an excuse! What about his treatment of Nettie, and his attitude toward women in general? When Shug finally arrives, he still treats Celie like a nonperson. Albert, moreover, is merely one of the many men in the film and the novel. What about all the rest?

What Alice Walker does is what all slave narratives do. Traditional narratives portray how personal behavior of masters and the personal life of slaves are located in a social context governed by the ideology of slavery and racism, which permeates every situation in the environment. They show, moreover, how the ideology of slavery and racism is supported and perpetuated by an ongoing Power Structure of *roles* and *offices.* Similarly, Alice Walker shows how sexist beliefs, ideas, attitudes and practices inhabit all spheres and aspects of life. In short, the ideology of sexism structures, institutionalizes, constitutes, and empowers itself both *as* patriarchy and *in* patriarchy.

[7]

The belief that men should be all-powerful and that women should be weak is at the foundation of all patriarchal ideology, which is clearly depicted in The Color Purple. Patriarchy is "good" because men are sacred, and matriarchy is "bad" because women are profane. This self-fulfilling dictum of the patriarchy is illustrated in the conspicuous absence of strong mother or grandmother figures, who are familiar personages in historical black communities.

Initially, Shug is perceived as a "wild" and "sinful" woman who later succumbs to a master-husband, and thereby acquiecses to patriarchy, in the form of her father. Sophia behaves "out of gender"—strong ("like a man")—and causes "trouble" and "divisiveness" in the normal patriarchal order of things. Walker does this so that we will not be confused as to the nature of patriarchy—how domineering, pervasive and exclusive male power is, or is supposed to be. After all, it is a patriarchal imperative that the male be, even as a child, the dominant sex. Accordingly, power is a taboo for women. Only males are supposed to possess, share and fight for power.

In The Color Purple, a gerontocracy obtains and a pecking order is established, with older males characteristically possessing most power and the younger ones having less power, but always aspiring to possess more. Differences exist in the workings of patriarchy in urban vis-à-vis rural environments. But in all patriarchies, so-called strong males dominate and serve as role models for so-called weaker ones. If the weaker ones do not turn into machos, they run the risk of being treated like "sissies" by their peers, and are "castrated" by them. In patriarchy, men (not women) "castrate" each other. With women supposedly completely out of the picture, patriarchy fosters an ongoing stepladder (hierarchy) between males possessing varying amounts and qualities of power. This is shown between Albert and his father; in turn, it is shown between Harpo and Albert; and, of course, between black men and white.

In The Color Purple, Harpo is put to instructive use. He is presented as an alternative contrast to the other men. Although he aspires to be the "boss," he is simply fated not to assume the role. He falls in love with a self-willed woman, Sophia, and fails miserably at trying to "tame" her. Despite the pressure put on him to be otherwise, it seems that Harpo is by nature a kind-hearted, non-macho and loving person. For this he was perceived as a "wimp" by nearly all who saw the film, including some women, which shows how effectively the macho values of patriarchy have been inculcated in us all. But, as is traditional in slave narratives, Harpo serves equally to provide "comic relief" from the many otherwise repulsive episodes. The buildup of tension found welcomed release in audiences across the nation at Harpo's bumbling attempts to be a macho man, like falling off the roof or getting beaten up by Sophia. Prolonged outbursts of cathartic laughter were enjoyed by all.

Because ownership, especially of money and property, is an essential ingredient of power, men own everything in The Color Purple. Albert is the prime example. He owns the money, the land, and what is produced on the land; he owns the house and the furnishings in the house. But the main thing about the proprietary claims of patriarchy is that men are supposed to own women and, therefore, men are supposed to own all that women might own themselves, including their very bodies, and especially their sex. The most ancient and prevalent patriarchal maxim is that men are master of all they survey. Female ownership of anything whatsoever is grievously frowned on and viewed as being an encroachment on the rights of men. When patriarchy is closely scrutinized, women are found to be divested of both the most trivial and fundamental rights, including ownership of themselves. From birth until they die, females are continuously owned by fathers, husbands, boyfriends, brothers, uncles or some man or another.

This is the situation with Celie, first owned by her father and later by Albert. Although she toils mightily in Albert's house and provides many services, including sex, she is penniless, and Albert treats her any way he chooses, because the overriding morality (ethics) of patriarchy toward women is that women have no rights that men are bound to respect. In the process, women are infantilized and rendered completely dependent on male paternalism for any kindness they might be accorded. The implied axiom here is that "Father knows best," or "men know what is best for women."

This aspect of patriarchy is epitomized in Albert's denial of Celie's right to privacy by withholding her letters, and is repeatedly portrayed in such acts as Albert slapping Celie for "talking back" ("sassing") him, and, of course, by regularly battering her—all done with utter impunity. He enters the kitchen and planks his muddy boot upon the table that Celie has labored to clean.

But the apex of patriarchal arrogance is represented by Albert's having Celie shave him, without the slightest consideration of how she must feel. In slavery, the feelings of the slave do not matter to the all-powerful master. Albert is so full of his power over Celie that he puts a razor in her hand and gives no thought as to whether she will shave his face or cut his throat, because in patriarchy, the man is lord and master. In patriarchy, women are supposed to be so cowed and brutalized by men's awesome power that they view themselves as nothing and view men as gods.

[8]

The connection between patriarchy and the idea of men as gods is a vital connection. God, religion and church are integral components of patriarchal ideology throughout the Christian world. This is particularly true in the case of fundamentalistic, tradition-bound religion, which is characteristically practiced by rural, peasant-type people, as portrayed in the film. This brand of religion and its churches are bulwarks of sexism and patriarchy. According to the Scriptures, God is not merely Jesus' father, but He is *the* Father. We pray, "Our Father who art in heaven." Hence, on the cross, Jesus cries out to his Father. In the Book of John, it is written that "the Spirit of truth . . . proceedeth from the Father."

All of this means that patriarchy consists of fathers and sons, with fathers passing on their power to the sons. In verse 17:1 of John, Jesus spake, "Father, the hour is come, glorify thy Son

. . . As thou has given him *power* over all flesh." In verse 15:1, the Son asserts "I am the true vine, and my Father is the husbandman." In verse 14:6, Jesus tightens the father-son power linkage by declaring that "no man cometh unto the Father, but by me." Notice also how it is written that God so loved the world he gave *not* his only daughter, but his only begotten Son. This is in keeping with the highest value being placed on fathers and sons by patriarchy and lowest value on mothers and daughters.

As mentioned above, on the cross Jesus cries out to his Father and not to his Mother. John 14:2 does not begin with Jesus saying "In my Mother's house are many mansions," but with him saying "In my Father's house are many mansions." Because, according to Protestant patriarchy, since we have no Mother in heaven, mothers are not supposed to own a house, let alone mansions.

Protestant Christianity, particularly as espoused by the apostle Paul, is one of the most patriarchal, woman-demeaning religions ever invented by men. The Twenty-third Psalm, for example, is the archcredo of patriarchal paternalism and phallic glorification: "The Lord is my shepherd . . . thy *rod* and thy *staff* they comfort me." This is the brand of religion most practiced by Southern blacks, whether they are actually in the South or in the North.

In patriarchy, then, all men are "fathers," i.e., patriarchs— they are lords and masters over women. It is only hinted at once in the book—in her letter to Celie, Shug refers to her parents as "mama and big daddy." But in the movie it is starkly brought out—Shug's father is the fiercely grim preacher patriarch. In fact, nearly all the men in the film, including Albert, look like preachers of one variety or another. According to church doctrine, preachers are God's representatives on earth. They are the Fathers of the Church and the Fathers of the Patriarchy. According to them, they are shepherds who have been ordained by God, the highest Father, to watch and rule over God's flock, meaning to rule society and specifically rule over women. The biblical mandate declares, "Slaves, obey your masters. . . . Wives, obey your husbands."

At best, in "chivalrous patriarchy," women are wards of men.

But, in fact, they are an oppressed *colony* at the disposal of the most powerful, oldest, richest, holiest and/or flamboyant men, especially the young women, the girls. When, for example, Celie finally liberates herself from Albert, his father tells him to get himself another slave for his house, "one of them young ones," to replace the slave he has lost. Celie was a slave. She worked like hell and did not receive "thanks," let alone any pay. When a man's home, apartment or room needs cleaning, organizing or beautifying, we do not advise the man to hire a maid or butler, we say he needs a wife, or, better yet, a "woman's touch." A female professor told a joke. She worked so hard teaching, being on committees, lecturing across the country, plus taking care of her own children and husband, cooking and doing housework for them, that one day she complained that what she needed was a *wife.*

[9]

As a sexist-patriarchal slave colony, women exist for the wanton exploitation of men in two primary modes: (1), women are free-for-all objects of exploitation as prostitutes in the public market of the street; (2) females are privately exploited as females—wives, daughters, nieces, et cetera in the family, or simply in the home or household. In both the novel and the film, the focus of The Color Purple is primarily on the home environment. In *Female Sexual Slavery,* Kathleen Barry says the slavery of women is a "family condition." She elaborates thusly:

> Female sexual slavery is present in *all* situations where women or girls cannot change the immediate conditions of their existence; where regardless of how they got into those conditions, they cannot get out; and where they are subject to sexual violence and exploitation . . . (p. 163)

In The Color Purple, novel and film, the specific details of this violence and exploitation are thoroughly portrayed in regard to all the women, but particularly in regard to Celie and Nettie. For Celie's father and for Albert, the home environment constitutes a privatized quarter of a colony of slaves. Similar to racist slavery, we see women and their children being sold, we

witness mere girls being examined and bargained for as property. As private property, rape and other crimes are perpetrated
against women at will. We see loved ones torn from each other,
just as in slavery, and sold away. There is the pathetic scene in
which Celie holds her baby in her arms in the town store, and
the pathos wells up in our throats. We think of the depiction of
this same sort of thing in poems written by Frances Harper over
a hundred years ago—"The Slave Mother" and "The Auction
Sale"—and similar scenes in dozens of slave narratives of those
times. We have recently read of such barbarity against black
women and their families in Margaret Walker's modern slave
narrative novel *Jubilee.*

During slavery, babies were born by girls who were babies
themselves, impregnated by slave masters and overseers. An
overseer rides along on a great horse. He sees a black slave girl
for whom he has had the "hots" for a long time. He proceeds to
rape her in the middle of a scenic field. The girl struggles to
fight him off, but he is stronger than she. There is no one to
help her.

[10]

Although we keep looking for the men in The Color Purple
to be white, they are black men, *our* men, committing deeds we
cannot help but associate with slavery. The analogy is unbearable, the irony is burning. Black men who are themselves victims of oppression victimizing black women with what looks
like the same oppression? A system of oppression within another system of oppression? We barricade our minds. The Color
Purple is "divisive" to black people, it portrays black men in a
"totally unacceptable" light. We believe with all our might that
it is *wrong* for Alice Walker to have done what she did. She did
exactly what is considered not "good" for black women to do.

[11]

But Alice Walker is merely one of many black women writing
in a similar vein today, notable among whom are Toni Morrison, Toni Cade Bambara, Ntozake Shange, Gayle Jones, Shirley

Ann Williams, and many more. The timeliest example is, of course, Gloria Naylor's *The Women of Brewster Place*, which was published the same year as *The Color Purple* (1982). What is more, in 1946, long before any of today's women began publishing, Ann Petry published her novel *The Street*, which contains all of the themes found in the writings of contemporary black women. Even before *The Street*, in 1937, Zora Neale Hurston, who is Walker's mentor, published *Their Eyes Were Watching God*, which was perhaps the first black womanist-oriented novel ever published. Alice Walker herself has published a lot of short stories and two other novels to date, my favorite of which is her first novel, *The Third Life of Grange-Copeland*. However, in both the film and the novel, the treatment of depth and scope is what makes The Color Purple outstanding and sets it apart from all similar works.

While it is a work of fiction modeled after the slave narrative and written in personal letters, with characters, scenes, and episodes, The Color Purple is one of the best sociological dramatic studies written on the subject of sexual oppression within the black race. It treats black female abuse as a generic function of sexism and patriarchy in black rural society and culture. Most significantly, the treatment portrays and depicts not merely the negative machinations of female oppression, it also dramatizes the positive process of growth and liberation.

[12]

Life for Celie may be visualized as an ever-expanding field of possibilities. In the center of this field is a great big mountain. It is the sexual mountain. Albert represents this mountain, which stands for all that is ugly and oppressive in women's lives. He and the mountain imprison Celie and prevent her from grasping any of life's potentialities.

On the other side of the mountain, the positive side, where the field beckons with opportunities for the development of life, is Shug Avery. Though she has not destroyed the mountain, she has scaled its repressive peaks of sexist bigotry and patriarchal domination. Breaking free of the fetters that would bind her down, she has been to the outside world and paid her dues. She has literally taken her life in her own hands and become a grown, independent woman who is terribly free. Her freedom is terrible, because, like most of her sex, she can be cut down at any moment by any number of forces seeking to put a woman like her in her "place." But she has taken her chances and survived so far.

Shug Avery is representative of the genre of black blues/jazz women who emerged during the beginning of the twentieth century. Similar to Bessie Smith, Mammy Yancey, Billie Holiday and uncounted others along city streets, in nightclubs and joints and in our prisons and graveyards, Shug Avery *is* the blues/jazz singer articulating the sorrows, brutalities, endurances and love-fleeting moments of all those women who, like Celie, are shackled down and rendered inarticulate in this woman-hating world. Shug feels her kinship with these women. Though they have been rendered divided into cliques and set to bickering among themselves on the basis of fat versus slim, black versus light-skinned and "pretty" versus "ugly," Shug knows that all women are sisters. This is what Shug brings to the scene. This is what the song she sings in the tavern—"Sister"— means. It is what all women need most in their lives, union, family, community—in a word, sisterhood. For only sisterhood, only togetherness, can effectively combat the awesome specter of the sexual mountain. And in this sense, Shug is Alice Walker's mouthpiece, she is Walker's womanist catalyst. Hazardous as it surely is, Shug is her own woman, i.e., she owns herself. She is therefore the most amazing female Celie has ever seen.

Celie is instantly fascinated by Shug. She has been expecting the "unknown quantity" whom Albert has pined for and upon whose arrival he turns into an ingratiating puppy. When the drunken, ill-tempered "wild woman" tells Celie she sure is one ugly child, she obviously means Celie no harm, and the slightly perturbed Celie cannot help grinning in amazement all the while. As she follows the action between Shug and Albert, you can hear Celie's thoughts—*Lord God Almighty! Whatever this woman is, I want to be some of her.* First, Shug shows Celie that there are other ways of being a woman beside being a child and a slave. Then Shug does something that nobody has ever done before: She stands up for Celie against the almighty "mister," she *befriends* Celie. The grin on Celie's face widens, becomes freer; behind her grin a glow begins to shine through. The subtlety, restraint and naturalness with which Whoopi Goldberg portrays Celie is all but imperceptible; she *is* Celie.

Ultimately Shug is totally admired by Celie, she looks up to Shug. She watches how Shug carries herself, how she dresses, curses and fraternizes with men as though they were mere people. She sees that anybody can cook. Or that anybody can try, even Albert. Most of all, Celie is fascinated by how womanish Shug is, and by how womanish she relates to Albert, whose name Celie learns for the first time.

But Celie does not come out of the deep hole in herself where she hides. The process of recovery from slavery is always slow and painful. There is no quick easy way. The slave mentality of a slave persists no matter whether the actual pressure has been lessened. Celie's interpretation of the situation—that Albert beats her because she is not Shug—is indicative of the gravity of the oppression under which she has been subjugated. Celie then does not think of growth, she thinks merely of escape, so the only idea she entertains is for Shug not to leave.

[13]

By now, though, in the novel, Shug has protected Celie in the tavern scene from Albert and from the heckling of the other women, and brought all the women together as sisters. She has also physically nurtured and loved Celie, she has brought out some of the woman so deeply repressed and undiscovered in Celie. Celie and Shug play in bed together, laugh together, and for the first time in her life Celie experiences joy. A woman deemed "ugly" means that she will be derided by both men and women, she will be ignored, rejected, hated by men and women. She will get to believe that she is indeed "ugly," and will come to accept what people deal out to her as perhaps her natural lot. But Shug Avery teaches and shows Celie that all beauty, and all ugliness, come from within.

In the novel, up to this time Celie has been writing to "Dear God." After she and Shug find Nettie's letters, she begins to write, "Dear Nettie." What Celie has been saying all along is,

"Dear Diary," or "Dear Journal," or, even more accurately, "Dear Slave Narrative." The change in the terms of address is a crucial statement. Celie is beginning to connect with specific human beings again. She is bridging the enforced gap with her estranged sister and ultimately with her family. Slowly, almost imperceptibly, the seed of growth is opening in her because of one person—Shug. Celie's change is happening because of one thing—love, both in the physical and the spiritual sense. Again, in the novel, Shug comes across as being a woman's woman, a lover and healer of women. This does not mean that she does not love men, because she does. It means that her heart is with women because she herself is a woman. She has no doubt been through the mill with all sorts of men and has experienced the school of hard knocks in the exigencies of life. She is like the character Mattie in Naylor's *Brewster Place,* or like at least one of the women about whom Toni Morrison writes in most of her books. Shug is an existential outsider, she is a woman-identified pansexual. She may bring you up or down, but you cannot reject her, cannot stop loving her, because you know she is on your side and will stand up for you even when you may not stand up for yourself or for her.

In the film, the lovemaking between Shug and Celie is omitted, save the kissing scene. The kissing, however, is done with such care and tenderness that it suffices to convey the meaning that Shug's love holds for Celie, and for the other women as well.

The dinner scene, for example, with all the men and all the women present, could not have come to pass without the influence and the love of Shug Avery. Because of Shug, Celie—and all the women—have moved from alienation and fragmentation to identity. By now, "Squeak" has stopped people from calling her "Squeak," and has asserted her real name, Mary Agnes. Celie and all the women have moved from dumbness to articulation, from weakness and subjugation to standing up to the supposedly all-powerful patriarchy. Celie has been fearfully shaving Albert as he dogs her. This same woman, who accepted a fist in her face for "sassing" her Mister, and who recommended a beating for one of her sisters, is now talking back. She is speaking out, not only to Albert, but to the entire patriarchy.

She and the women, moreover, do what women are never supposed to do—*laugh* at men. The women have learned, largely from Shug, that when women come together, the sexual mountain is not infallible. Besides, like her mentor, Celie is now at the stage where she does not give a damn. She is not going to be a slave anymore. Thus the most significant act of Celie's transformation comes with the commandeering of a knife in defense of herself and her sister, Sophia, who started out as the indomitable strong woman.

[14]

With minor exceptions, such as the age difference, Sophia is reminiscent of the familiar black-woman personage so faithfully portrayed and celebrated by Langston Hughes, the independent, self-made, strong-willed Madam Alberta K. Johnson. Both mentally and physically, she is built for defending herself. She is a solid woman with a strong sense of integrity, unpretentious, and she is likeable.

In the context, it is amusing that Harpo, although a good-enough fellow, is simply no equal to Sophia either in personal or physical qualities. Harpo wants to be like the rest of the men. It is all he knows because it is all he has seen around him. After all, his daddy and granddaddy are little more than macho barbarians. Since Harpo is really a teenager, and little in size, he is bulldozed and intimidated by his father, Albert. It is then Sophia who stands up to Albert, rather than Harpo. Harpo has no other role models, no other socializing agents, except his father and the others who are all sexists of the most fundamentalist type. However, since Sophia will have none of this, Harpo is at his wit's end during the first half of The Color Purple.

But if one mountain does not get the black woman, another mountain will, the racial mountain. The town scene is gruesome and painful, because we are forced to witness how a strong black woman, stranded alone, can be broken by racist and sexist violence of white men, and by white women. Precisely because of her integrity and penchant for self-defense, Sophia is set upon by white Southern racists. Cowed, the black people mill around, looking on. This is before Shug has catalyzed them to transform themselves from fragmentation to union based on equality and love between women and women, as well as between women and men. Imprisoned for defending herself and made to suffer the draconian irony of slaving for the very "cracker woman" who started it all in the first place, Sophia is brought low, much lower than even Celie who was delivered into wretchedess at birth.

Alice Walker is taking us inside the very process in and through which human beings are transformed, both for the worse and for the better. We started with Celie already in a state of utter degradation and meticulously followed her, and all the women, through the process of changing for the better. Then Walker reverses this process with Sophia. We are familiar with how prisoners are broken down in a long, tedious process of torture, and made to confess anything and do anything. Racism from white men and women, and sexism from white men, and then another sexism from black men constitute a societal and cultural torture of geometric intensity that every black woman experiences too many times, if not constantly, in her life. Although Sophia is able to handle sexism from black men, we witness all the rest happen to her in one blow, in the town scene. Later, when she is released, looking twice her age, we are touched in our deep places, and we readily share her gloom and spiritual angst.

But just in case we mistakenly conclude that black women's suffering is due only to racism and sexism of whites, Sophia and the whites are removed from the scene while we witness Celie undergo the same type of torture at the hands of black men. Walker shows us that inequality and brutality against black women are an issue in the black family itself, and in the black community at large. Sophia has told us herself that "a girl ain't safe in a house full of menfolks." This is why it is no accident that Albert and Shug have been lovers and that Albert remains involved with her, because at its core The Color Purple is an affair of the black family, an affair that is always connected with and usually includes the whole black community. Most of all, what Sophia's situation shows is that no amount of strength and integrity on the part of the individual alone can effectively overcome the coordinated violence of a system.

The re-transformation of Sophia into her true self again is brought about in and by the collective sisterhood of black women, at the dinner scene, and specifically by the acts of Celie, the *new* Celie. Notice the reversal of the conditions of these two women. At the dinner table, particularly in the film, Celie is now where Sophia was in the beginning, and Sophia is where Celie was. Somebody asks Sophia how she feels. "Confused" is the mumbled reply. She has been stripped of her identity and reduced to a dejected nonentity. But Sophia is gathered up in the new spirit of Celie and the women, much like Shug gathered Celie in her arms, and Sophia is rejuvenated and grounded with her sisters. She is, in the integrity of the meaning, born again. But this time Sophia is born into a family of women who love her. Even before Nettie and children return, Celie and the women literally take back from the men their family, the very name of which the men had persistently abused and profaned.

[15]

The porch scene is the culmination of the tedious process of transformation into liberation. It is the climactic crystalization of all the positive elements in the film, and it is the most captivating, the most powerful image of all. Facing the screen from the audience, Celie is on the left in back, and Mary Agnes ("Squeak") is exactly in line about four yards across from Celie, with Shug about fifteen paces up front in the center position. They are on the porch of the house that Celie just inherited, which belonged to her all along, but which her father (stepfather) had stolen from her. Trees hover about the porch in full bloom and the wind is gently blowing. The three women are standing tall, facing boldly out at the audience and the world. They are not a triangle, not a "matriarchy"; rather, they are a diamond, they are at once a metaphor and a paradigm. In togetherness, in struggle, in love, they have triumphed. In the process they have transformed themselves from isolated nonentities to a family of sisters, they have come from colony to community, from slaves to free women. They are womanish women. The energy flowing between and emanating from them is pure radiance.

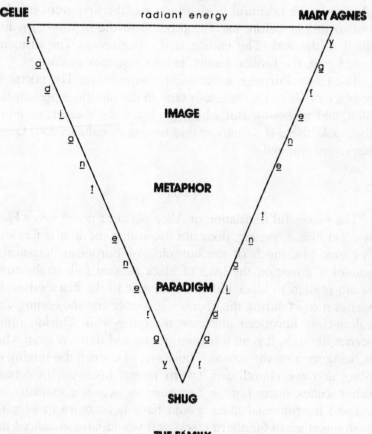

THE PORCH SCENE
THE DIAMOND OF WOMEN IN SISTERHOOD

CELIE   radiant energy   MARY AGNES

r   y

a   g

d   r

i   a

IMAGE

a   n

n   e

t   n

METAPHOR

t   n

e   e

n   i

PARADIGM   i

e   r

n   g

e   a

i   r

r   y

g   a

y   r

SHUG

THE FAMILY

THE COMMUNITY

**THE
WORLD**

The female symbol of the porch scene foliates the portent of its harvest into the pastoral pathos of a happy ending. Like the opening scene, the closing scene is idyllic, homespun and lyrical. Along with the music, it is a pastoral that consummates the opening scene at the very beginning where Celie and Nettie are playing in the beautiful field, which was the first motif in what was to unfold before us. The promise in the beginning is fulfilled in the end. The ending is the beginning. The dismembered tree, the broken family, is back together again.

The Color Purple is a demanding experience. The portrayal of black males can leave a sour taste in the mouth, especially for men, and it should. But when you leave the theater, or finish the book, there is an inescapable feeling of exhilaration. Good has overcome evil.

[16]

The successful translation of Alice Walker's novel into a Hollywood film, however, does not mean that the film is flawless. For example, much of the imposing of European "classical"-sounding music on the lives of black peasant folk in the rural South is alien to black life and antithetic to the black ethos. In scenes such as during the opening sequence and the ending, the ruling-class European music works quite well. During other scenes, though, it is an intrusion, it jars and detracts from what is being seen on the screen. There are, of course, the singing of Shug and the church and tavern music. Likewise, in certain other scenes, instead of the European music, some thematic vocal and instrumental blues would have been more in keeping with the ethos of Southern blacks and would have enhanced the mood of those scenes.

Secondly, in the novel the making of the pants and the interaction between Celie, Shug, Mary Agnes, and the other women, girls and men, including Albert, in Memphis show a crucial phase in the furtherance of the independent development of Celie as a woman, and of Albert as a less-sexist man. The process of Celie's continued growth and sisterhood building is skipped over in the movie. Only the "comic" side of Harpo trying on a pair of the "unisex" pants is portrayed.

Thirdly, as mentioned earlier, not in the novel but in the film, there is the unexplained paradox in the way Albert relates to Celie vis-à-vis the way he relates to Shug, which lends itself to possible misinterpretation as to who's to blame for Celie's wretchedness under Albert. Since Shug will not accept meanness from Albert, it may be inferred that Albert treats Celie meanly because she, unlike Shug, does not demand respect from him. But when we consider the common "exception" practice of slave masters catering to a "favorite" black while lynching all the rest, Albert's behavior toward Shug is clearly the personal exception; whereas his ways toward Celie and Nettie are not personal at all, but are reflective of the patriarchal relations that are supposed to exist between all men and women, including the exceptions.

The change that comes over Albert toward the end of the film may be interpreted in a similar light. The kindness he shows and the money he uses to pay for Nettie's and Celie's children to come from Africa are but drops in the bucket compared to what he really owes Celie for the years of free labor and personal services she has provided him. In the movie, there is no real indication that Albert has grown. His consciousness has not been raised. Aging and alone, he merely drops out, without any sense that his brutal feelings and actions have been reflective of a system of sexism and patriarchy in which they all live. Whatever saving grace his later actions signify in the movie, they come too late. While Albert's actions may be appreciated, the way they are presented in the movie, they appear to be more of a cop-out than anything else.

On the other hand, in the novel itself, the notion of Albert "mellowing with age" is treated in much more detail over a longer period of time and is rather convincingly portrayed. Walker has been criticized by younger men for her tendency to show men in a better light once they have aged. After Celie moves to Memphis, and while Shug is away on tours, Albert and Celie have many conversations. He actually begins to listen to the new womanish Celie, and gradually begins to change his sexist beliefs, feelings and behavior. More and more he relates to Celie as an equal and she relates to him as sort of his mentor. She, for example, teaches him to sew. They both love the same woman, Shug—and they begin to have a buddy relationship in which Celie even comes to feel just a hint of sexual awakening for her ex-master who is now her pupil and is showing substantial signs of becoming a new man.

Along with Harpo's desire but inability to be a macho man, I have already mentioned the "passive" sexism of Shug's men friends in the movie version of Walker's novel. Shug's men, including her husband, sort of linger innocuously about, grinning and waiting to do Shug's bidding. Their attitude is typified by the attitude of the ex-boxer who comes to the tavern with Sophia and tells Harpo that he does not fight Sophia's battles. "My job is to love her and take her where she wants to go." To the extent that these men are relatively less violent and hateful than Albert and his father and Celie's and Shug's fathers, they may be considered good men. But, in the movie portrayal of them, they do nothing toward eradicating the sexist system that supposes men as bosses over women. Again, on the other hand, particular in the last third of the book, in addition to the transformation taking place in Albert, Walker portrays Shug's men friends, along with other men such as Odessa's husband, Jack, as being more actively supportive of the ideas and behaviors of equality and togetherness between women and men.

Another possible cop-out, not only in the film but in the novel as well, concerns how the matter of incest is handled. In both the novel and film, we find out toward the end that Celie was not raped by her real father, it was only her stepfather. Are we therefore supposed to breathe a sigh of relief? In sexist-intensive situations such as Celie's in The Color Purple, it matters not one iota—whether daughters, stepdaughters, sisters, nieces, wives or whoever—sexual abuse of women, and young girls in particular, is a de facto part of the rights and rites of patriarchy carried on in the household. This is true in practice despite the most adamant disclaimers and proclamations of moral taboo. The remark made by the girl Daisy, whom Celie's stepfather "marries" later on, is a telling remark. Celie asks Daisy how the aged stepfather died, and Daisy replies, "On top of me."

But these flaws, cop-outs, and inconsistencies in either or both the novel and the film are rather minor and do not threaten the integrity of the film and certainly not the novel. There are two flaws, though, that warrant major concern. One of them occurs in both the film and the novel; the other occurs only in the film.

[17]

The first pertains to the African sequences. In the novel, I think Walker wanted to show the connection between culture in Africa and culture in the American South, and show that, although influenced by the American system, black sexism harks back all the way to Africa. Walker also intended for the African sequences to add scope and depth to Nettie's maturing process as reflected in her letters.

In slave narratives, the slave would escape to the North (which was like being in another country) and engage in humanitarian work, broadening and deepening his or her awareness, and this work and new awareness would impact one way or another on the situation in the South.

But in The Color Purple, the movie and the novel, the African sequences and the letters are extraneous and take away from the flow of what is happening on the home front. We need to know what is happening to Nettie's and Celie's children. But the sequences of African scenes in the film are too ethereal and shabby. The surreal interpositioning of the African scarification ceremony with Celie shaving Mister is like putting Sunday school and a burning bed in the same picture. The two realities are mixed, like a mixed metaphor, and do not convey a coherent and meaningful image. Then, too, there are not enough African people to give a real sense of being in Africa; instead, the shots of jungle animals in a vacant landscape and the dreamlike quality of the scenes are like celluloid postcards of unreality.

In the novel itself, the *writing* of the letters is incongruous with the texture and substance of Celie's narrative. The style and temperament of Nettie's letters, moreover, sound too much as if they were written during the nineteenth century by, say, Charlotte Forten Grimke. While Nettie's letters provide needed information, the African correspondence is simply too much of a departure from the slave-narrative genre in which the rest of *The Color Purple* is decidedly written. It is the way in which Walker includes this material that makes for a serious fracture in the slave-narrative form as *genre*. Unlike Celie's letters, the writing of Nettie sounds too much like the stylized rendering of a middle-class romantic-heroine do-gooder.

But the most offensive breach from *The Color Purple* as novel occurs in the movie version's portrayal of Shug. In the novel, and for most of the film, Shug Avery is a blues/jazz woman, and a pansexual. The last part of the film, however, completely emaciates this view of her. Toward the end we see this bold, independent woman turned into nothing more than her daddy's little girl. The message here is altogether recognizable. Shug, the liberated woman, the "lesbian," the would-be revolutionary, is thoroughly discredited. All along she has been motivated, not by her womanish integrity, but by a "Freudian complex" covertly desiring her father's love and acceptance—that hardened traditionalist, patriarchal preacher father who disowns his daughter and refuses to acknowledge her very existence. "Look, look," Shug cries out to him, "I am *married!*" She holds out her finger to show him the ring, *proof* of her "heterosexualism," *symbol* of her being owned by a man! Her hard-won independence, her blues/jazz flamboyance, her revolutionary ways and potential are suddenly shown to be nothing but "adolescent rebellion" against her father. In the novel, not even a question of Shug's validity is ever hinted at. She continues to grow even more womanish, and her spirit impacts increasingly on Celie and everyone, including Albert. But in the movie her character is totally mutilated. This is by far the biggest capitulation to patriarchy, the most dastardly cop-out in the film, and the most blatant reversal of what happens in the novel.

[18]

Despite these major flaws, both the film and the novel stand up remarkably well, they remain unscathed before the acrimonious onslaught leveled against them. Below are some key examples of the accusations raised against Alice Walker and her book:

1. Negative, stereotypical portrayal and images of black men;
2. No strong black male role models depicted, an unbalanced treatment of black men;
3. Does not depict racism and white hatred and oppression causing black males to behave the way they do toward black women;
4. Negative implications for the black family similar to the infamous Moynihan Report;
5. Walker should not have aired "dirty laundry" before the eyes of white people who will use The Color Purple to justify their genocide against the black race;
6. The movie should never have gotten nominated for any awards. It should have gotten the award since it was nominated;
7. The Color Purple, movie and book, received too much publicity from whites, therefore something must be wrong. Alice Walker rose too quickly to fame in the eyes of white people and was embraced by white feminists;
8. It was all Spielberg's fault, a white man's conspiracy against black people;
9. Too much lesbianism, not enough lesbianism;
10. Nobody knows any black people like those portrayed in the film, beyond imagination, not believable, false depiction, unrealistic.

The people who put forth these and other accusations were largely intellectuals, writers, critics, politicos and race leaders, among whom black men cried out the loudest and most damning. In 1986, for example, a "Black Man Think Tank" convened at the University of Cincinnati. On their list of topics for discussion was "Will The Color Purple Destroy The Color Black?" Forums, conferences, debates and random meetings were held in black communities across the nation. Uncountable reviews, essays and articles were written. Talk shows and special television programs were devoted to the controversy. The NAACP denounced it. Picketing and demonstrations were carried out in most major cities as well as in remote corners of the country. A cacophony of palavar and a whirlwind of emotions were let loose.

But in all of it there was nothing new, nothing different from what had happened in both the distant as well as the recent past. From its inception during the eighteenth century, Afro-American writing has always been the object of heated controversy on the part of both white and black people. Phillis Wheatley, Jupiter Hammon, Paul Laurence Dunbar, Jessie Fauset, Zora Neale Hurston and every black writer worth a piece of paper and a pencil have been the object of assault from some segment of the black population at one time or another. All writers who are members of a historically oppressed group of people are necessarily subject to controversy from their own people. No matter what you say in your work, or do not say, somebody is going to find fault with it. Female or male, controversy comes with the territory of being a black writer. This is especially true if the writer happens to write something that "makes it big." Instantly the writer is accused of "selling out," accused of stereotyping, accused of an unbalanced portrayal, accused of deserting his or her people, accused of one fault or another: Langston Hughes, Ann Petry, Richard Wright, James Baldwin, Ralph Ellison, Margaret Walker, Robert Hayden, John A. Williams, Ntozake Shange, Michele Wallace, Ishmael Reed, Toni Morrison, Audre Lorde, Amiri Baraka, and on and on. While one segment of the black population might praise a certain aspect of your work, another segment will damn you for the same aspect.

During the 1920s, the first black literary and cultural movement in America tried to grapple with this problem, this unyielding albatross around the necks of black writers. A symposium was conducted in the pages of *Crisis* magazine under the editorship of W. E. B. Dubois. The symposium was entitled "The Negro: How Shall He Be Portrayed?" Seven questions were asked:

1. When the artist, black or white, portrays Negro characters, is he under any obligations or limitations as to the sort of character he will portray?

2. Can any author be criticized for painting the worst or the best characters of a group?

3. Can publishers be criticized for refusing to handle novels that portray Negroes of education and accomplishment, on the

ground that these characters are no different from white folk and therefore not interesting?

4. What are Negroes to do when they are continually painted at their worst and judged by the public as they are painted?

5. Does the situation of the educated Negro in America with its pathos, humiliation and tragedy call for artistic treatment at least as sincere and sympathetic as "Porgy" received?

6. Is not the continued portrayal of the sordid, foolish and criminal among Negroes convincing the world that this and this alone is really and essentially Negroid, and preventing white artists from knowing any other types and preventing black artists from daring to paint them?

7. Is there not a real danger that young colored writers will be tempted to follow the popular trend in portraying Negro character in the underworld rather than seeking to paint the truth about themselves and their own social class?

The public was invited to respond to the questions, including writers, painters, editors, publishers, men, women, whites and blacks. While certain people agreed on some of the questions, other respondents took different sides on each of the questions, and there was no unanimous agreement on any of them.

The bricks and arrows hurled at Alice Walker and her novel are motivated by the same old concern as to how the black writer should portray black people. People from different backgrounds with different sensitivities, ideologies and class leanings will respond differently to the same work. Jealousy and envy are also a part of the motivations. However, more than with any other black-authored work so far, The Color Purple seemed to have driven some of its critics literally *crazy.* Tony Brown was the most glaring example. Declaring that he had not seen the film nor read the book and would never do so, he published several articles in the black press and devoted more than one of his weekly syndicated *Tony Brown's Journal* television shows to the subject. He ranted and raved against Walker, Spielberg and the film. He accused Whoopi Goldberg of not qualifying as a black actress. To the people who objected to his denunciations of The Color Purple, he wrote in the March 3, 1986, issue of the Cleveland *Call And Post* that they were "frustrated Black women, closet homosexual men; closet lesbians; and meddling white people."

While Tony Brown and hordes of other such black men (and some women) were condemning The Color Purple as being the "most savage treatment of Black men since *Birth of a Nation,*" I received a letter from a Georgia black woman, in which she wrote the following:

> The article I wrote was on sexually abused children. Last August, four cases were tried locally concerning children that had been sexually abused. In three of the four cases, the victims were black and they were cases of incest. . . . Shortly after this, a black female and her common-law preacher/husband were arrested for physically and sexually abusing the woman's five year old daughter. . . . I was so horrified by this and the previous cases that I decided to investigate child sex abuse in the black community.
>
> To my surprise, most of the lay people felt that it was something that I shouldn't write about, keep it in the dark. Others thought it only happened in white families. . . . I talked with a succession of women who had been either abused by their natural fathers or by their step-fathers. One woman was still caught in her father's web and she was thirty years old. Several agreed to tell their stories, but shortly before my deadline everyone of them backed out except one. I went ahead with the series with the hope of opening someone's eyes to what is going on and hopefully getting something done about the problem.
>
> All of this brings me to Alice Walker's book, *The Color Purple.* I think she did a damn good job. Knowing my family's background, I could easily say she wrote about us.
>
> If I can give you any information on battered black women, I can write a book giving plenty insight on what it feels like to be one.
>
> Sincerely,
>
> Catharine _____

Despite the volume of negative fireworks aimed at The Color Purple, and despite Tony Brown, who took credit for turning people against it, hundreds of thousands of black people bought the book and packed the movie houses across the nation. Tens of thousands of boys and girls, as well as older people, went to see the film and purchased the book, some of whom were seventy and eighty years old and had not been to the theater in many years. Thousands more saw the film two and even three times over.

So who's afraid of Alice Walker, who's afraid of The Color Purple?

POSTSCRIPT

Another telling commentary on the clang of fury leveled against *The Color Purple* is the volume of silence that *The Women of Brewster Place* has received. *The Women of Brewster Place*, a first novel by Gloria Naylor, was published during the same time as was *The Color Purple*. It, too, was awarded a prestigious American literary prize. It, too, was on the best-seller list. It, too, is a womanist feminist novel. In many ways, Naylor's novel is a more exacting depiction of the sexism of black men than is *The Color Purple*. *The Women of Brewster Place* might also contain a greater degree of artistic daring, plus woman-identified bonding and nurturing ("lesbianism"), than what is found in Walker's novel. Why the silence? Is it because Naylor's novel has not made as much money as *The Color Purple* and not received as much publicized acclaim from the white world, specifically from white feminists? Is it because *Brewster Place* has not been made into a "box-office success" by a big-time Hollywood director? Furthermore, do critics of Alice Walker actually believe that a whitewashed presentation of black people in art will change the way racist white people think and behave toward black people? Are there black women and men who fear what whites might think of them more than they care about the revelation of the truth? Can it be that the homophobic, nitpicking screams of denial against The Color Purple are motivated out of envy, jealousy and guilt, rather than out of any genuine concern for the well-being of black people? None of Alice Walker's critics, moreover, has uttered a word about the practice of woman battering that pervades our culture, as portrayed in the television presentation of *The Burning Bed.*

Does all of this silence say something about the humanity of not only Walker's critics but about the humanity of us all?

TWO

The Sexual Mountain and Black Women Writers

> We younger Negro artists who create now intend to express our individual dark-skinned selves without fear or shame. If white people are pleased—we are glad. If they are not, it doesn't matter. We know we are beautiful. And ugly too. The tom-tom cries and the tom-tom laughs. If colored people are pleased we are glad. If they are not, their displeasure doesn't matter either. We build our temples for tomorrow, strong as we know how, and we stand on top of the mountain, free within ourselves.
>
> —LANGSTON HUGHES, "The Negro Artist and The Racial Mountain"

From the beginning black writers have written a literature of social protest and human enlightenment—and black writing has always been under siege. During 250 years of slavery, it was a legal crime for blacks to read and write. Frederick Douglass risked his life and his sight trying to learn how to read in darkness by a candle in the forest. The slave Jupiter Hammon had to limit his writing according to what his master would tolerate. David Walker, a free black, was murdered for what he wrote. None of the early writers sat in ivory towers surrounded by fetishes of refined culture and composed "art for art's sake."

Black writing did not come into being as a result of some black person's desire to exercise the "inspirational muse." What motivated blacks to write was the condition of oppression, and what they desired of their writing was for it to ameliorate their condition.

Black people, moreover, including the writers themselves, have summoned and even harassed black writers to report on and define the condition of the race and its struggle. Since writers possess the Word and the Word is Powerful, the people feel it is the inherent duty of writers to communicate the wishes of the people and, if need be, lead the people against those who oppress them. By virtue of its origin, nature and function, black writing is *mission-conscious* and is necessarily a hazardous undertaking. In turn, being a black writer is an ennobling exigency, and black literature constitutes one of the supreme enrichments of black culture and black life. This has been and is the burden as well as the heritage and the legacy of every black person who takes up the pen in the United States.

It is therefore a mean irony and a down-right shame that the men authors and gate-keepers of Black American Literature have historically ignored, belittled and suppressed the women authors and the works they have produced. Historically, the battle line of the racial struggle in the United States has been drawn exclusively as a struggle between the men of the races. Everything having to do with race has been defined and counter-defined by the men as a question of whether black people were or were not a race of Men. The central concept and the universal metaphor around which all aspects of the racial situation revolve is "Manhood." Whatever whites have done to blacks, it is viewed, by the men, not as the wronging of an entire people, males and females. Rather, it is viewed solely in terms of the denial of the MANHOOD of a people. The situation boils down to: no matter what shape the world is in, it is never supposed to be a woman's world, it is always a MAN'S world. Although black and white men stand on opposing sides of the racial mountain in America, they tread on common ground when it comes to the mountain of sex.

Traditionally, the World of Black Literature in the United States has been a world of black men's literature. The "fathers" and purveyors of black writing have been men. There have been no recognized "mothers" of black literature. From the eighteenth-century manuscript of Olaudah Equiano to Alex Haley's *Roots,* the narrative works receiving the most attention have been authored by men. From Jupiter Hammon's "Address to the Negroes of the State of New York" to the "I Have a Dream" speech by Martin Luther King, the remembered quotations, essays, polemics and scholarly writings have been authored by men. The male authors have portrayed male heroes and male protagonists almost exclusively, and the complexity and vitality of black female experiences have been fundamentally ignored.

Consider, for example, the depiction of black women in the two most acclaimed black novels of the twentieth century. In *Native Son,* Richard Wright portrays Bigger Thomas's mother and sister "realistically" as decrepit nagging bitches. Bigger's girlfriend, Bessie Mears, is a pathetic nothing. Mary Rambo, the black female in Ralph Ellison's *Invisible Man,* is a symbolic mammy figure; early in the novel there is a contributory poetic passage which refers to another female folk personage, "Mother Gresham." James Baldwin is the only superstar black male novelist who rather persistently portrays black women as persons largely in their own right. It is a matter of historical record that, until recently, black writing in the United States has been systematically discriminatory against black women.

Black women have been involved in the development of Afro-American writing since its inception, yet no pre-twentieth-century black women writers are treated as major contributors to the history of black literature. The back-burner status of female writers persists into the twentieth century too. Despite women writers such as Effie Lee Newsome, Georgia Douglas Johnson, Anne Spencer, Alice Dunbar-Nelson, Nella Larson, Jessie Fauset, Dorothy West, Helene Johnson, and others, it has been almost impossible to read the critical works and general history of the New Negro/Harlem Renaissance of the 1920s and get any impression other than that the "New Negroes" were entirely of the male sex. The only female of the period to receive substantial recognition is Zora Neale Hurston—but only as an "oddball" eccentric who wrote folktales and ran around measuring Negroes' heads. Until recently Hurston's most significant books, *Their Eyes Were Watching God* and *Jonah's Gourd Vine*, were neglected.

Despite the legacy of this double standard—lack of equal reward for equal work—black women, like black men, continued to write throughout the Depression years on into the 1960s. But unlike men, some of whom rose to heights of literary dominance, the women received the usual secondary treatment. *Native Son* (1940), devoted to the plight of America's black male youth, was and is hailed as a masterpiece, and has remained in-print. Ann Petry's 1946 novel *The Street*, devoted to the tragedy of a young black female who is crippled, exploited, and driven to murder by the oppressive misogynous systems of the white *and* black man, seems always to be out-of-print. Unlike Wright's fiction, Petry's work has, until recently, been known by only a small number of blacks (and whites) since the 1950s.

The same situation has prevailed regarding the works of other black women writers whose female protagonists stand as timeless examples of the autonomous humanity of their sex, such as the transplanted West Indian women in Paule Marshall's *Brown Girl, Brownstones*, Merle Kinbona in Marshall's *The Chosen Place, The Timeless People*, Mariah Upshur in Sarah Wright's *This Child's Gonna Live*, Lena, Beneatha, and Ruth in Lorraine Hansberry's *A Raisin in the Sun*, and Vyry in Margaret Walker's *Jubilee*, the first contemporary slave-narrative novel.

Except for Gwendolyn Brooks, and perhaps Margaret Walker, the name of not one black woman writer and not one female protagonist was accorded a worthy status in the black literary world prior to the 1970s, not even Hansberry, first black woman to have a play on Broadway. Gwendolyn Brooks *was* the exception. Her age, her numerous prizes and awards and honors from the white literary world, the prestige she *already* had, plus her unquestionable genius, made her, *per force*, the acceptable exception.

Although the 1960s witnessed a plethora of black female writers, especially poets, the legacy of male chauvinism in the black literary world continued to predominate. In fact, during the Black Power/Black Arts Movement of the 1960s, the unequal recognition and treatment of women writers was enunciated more bigotedly than perhaps ever before. "The only position in the revolution for women is the prone position!" "The women's place is seven feet behind the men!" Pronouncements like these were reflected again and again in the writings, and deeds, of the males of the period. In Stokely Carmichael and Charles Hamilton's *Black Power, The Politics of Liberation in America*, not one black woman is mentioned significantly, not even Angela Davis. In Harold Cruse's encyclopedia masterpiece, *The Crisis of the Negro Intellectual*, about thirty women are mentioned, largely in passing, most of whom are entertainers such as Josephine Baker and Lena Horne. There also occurred, if one remembers, the proliferation of macho pimp films and books, *Superfly, Sweetback, Shaft, Nigger Charlie;* Nathan Heard's *Howard Street* and Iceberg Slim's autobiographical works enjoyed lively sales. During the heyday, moreover, of the Black Power Black Revolution Black Arts Movement, one could go through the Black Studies Curriculum and learn all about the Black Experience, and encounter less than a handful of black females. The first issue of the *Black Scholar* magazine came out in 1969. The issue was entitled, "The Culture of Revolution." Nine articles were listed in the table of contents. All of them were authored by men. On the inside cover the editorial states:

> . . . A black scholar . . . is a man of both thought and action, a whole man who thinks for his people and acts with them, a man who honors the whole community of black experience, a man who sees the Ph.D., the janitor, the businessman, the maid, the clerk, the militant, as all sharing the same experience of blackness, with all its complexities and its rewards. THE BLACK SCHOLAR is the journal for such a man.*

Precisely, black men have historically defined themselves as sole interpreters of the Black Experience. They have set the priorities, mapped out the strategies, and sought to enforce the rules. Yet, as in the past, black women during the 1960s doggedly continued to write. Similar to the great number of male writers, there were more women writers than ever before. They

---

* Changes in the editorial personnel of the *Black Scholar* since the first issue, plus the raising of consciousness, brought about a more egalitarian policy toward women that has become evident in subsequent issues.

found publishers and got read. They made recordings of their works, which sold in the tens of thousands. Many of them took to the road, lecturing and reading. A number of them achieved unprecedented recognition. Unmistakably, the recognition was achieved because black women, particularly the poets, constituted a formidable phalanx of the conscious-raising activities of the 1960s. The macho philosophy of the Black Power Black Arts Movement resulted in so many demeaning experiences for the women, that many of them began to protest and eventually break away. Older women who had been raising children and servicing husbands all of their lives, Sarah Webster Fabio, for example, began actualizing their talent. In the process they became peers and teachers of the young. Activists, students and lone sideliners alike, all joined in what was now a more thorough consciousness of themselves as Black Women. Then, in 1970, Toni Cade Bambara published an anthology, *The Black Woman,* in which twenty-seven women writers expressed, according to the jacket notes, "the rising demand by women for liberation from their chattel-like roles in a male-dominated society." Significantly, a preponderance of the writers had backgrounds in the Civil Rights *cum* Black Power Movement. It was this anthology that signaled the decline of the historical inequality of women writers in Afro-American Literature.

[2]

Today, the women of the 1960s are writing in an increasingly pioneer fashion, among whom are Audre Lorde, June Jordan, Vertamae Smart-Grosvenor, Jayne Cortez, Maya Angelou, Ann Shockley, Sonia Sanchez, Alice Walker, Toni Cade Bambara. There are "Old Timers" who were writing before the 1960s, such as Paule Marshall, Gwendolyn Brooks, Margaret Walker, Margaret Danner, and Sarah Wright, who broke ground for the generation of the 1960s, and who are now griots of song and letters, foremothers of ancient testament and new truths. There are also the "late bloomers" who were around during the 1960s and 1970s, but are just now coming into publication, as represented by Barbara Masekela, Hattie Gossett, Regina Williams and Barbara Christian. Altogether, these women are now in league with a prodigious progeny of new black women authors. The new, younger women are scaling the traditional sexual mountain of Afro-American Literature with an avalanche of explosive writings. Thylias Moss, Donna Kate Rushin, Hillary Kay, Cheryle Jones, Gloria Hull, Patricia Jones, Shirley Ann Williams, Pat Parker, Lorraine Bethel, Stephanie Byrd, Michelle Cliff, to mention but a few. There is a freshness of style, sensitivity and language, a boldness of subject and stance, and a newness of treatment imbued with exciting promise. The writings of these women, and many more like them, constitute the celebration of the black women's literary Fourth of July for the first time in the United States.

Though Bambara's *The Black Woman* anthology in 1970 heralded the weakening of male literary dominance over females, it was not until 1978 that the straw which actually broke the billy goat's back appeared in the form of the Broadway production of Ntozake Shange's *For Colored Girls Who Have Considered Suicide When the Rainbow Is Enuf.* In fact, there were two straws, the second being the 1979 publication of Michele Wallace's book, *Black Macho and the Myth of the Super Woman.*

Hell broke loose.

Black males took severe offense over the rave reviews Shange's *Colored Girls* received from the critics who, the blacks said, were mostly Jewish males. Shange, the black men said, was a goddamn traitor to the race. In a time when black men were striving for respect, here comes some middle class, light skin bitch, putting black men down before the eyes of the white world. Resentment was also expressed over Shange's quick rise to fame—off of a bullshit, nothing ass recitation of some fucking man-hating poems! Nothing but a rip-off. That's all it was, the men said.

The air had not begun to clear over *Colored Girls* when *Ms.* hit the newsstands with pre-publication excerpts of *Black Macho,* announcing on the cover that Wallace's book would determine the central issue for blacks during the 1980s. A few days later the book topped the bestseller list. The same feelings black men expressed about *Colored Girls* were expressed about *Black Macho,* only more of them and much stronger, including a noticeable number of black women writers, intellectuals and political activists. Dissent and controversy reigned. June Jordan reviewed *Macho* in the New York *Times* Book Review—it was not favorable. Jordan seemed outraged over the *Ms.*'s assertion that *Macho* would sound the main issue for blacks in the 1980s. Wallace was to be interviewed by Jordan on a New York Radio station. But, according to her sister who phoned the station, Wallace became paranoid en route and never arrived.

The mobilization against Wallace, and in the process Shange too, was quick and solid. It came from all sectors of the black population, the press, the literary and scholarly journals and magazines, and on black and white college campuses, and in the ghettoes as well. Wallace and Shange were invalidated as writers, scholars, and most of all they were put down as black women. Vernon Jarret, in the *Chicago Defender*, equated Shange's play with "that classic pro–Ku Klux Klan achievement of 1915, 'Birth of a Nation'!" Jarret went on to assert that *Colored Girls* was "a degrading treatment of the black male . . . a mockery of the black family." Stanley Crouch wrote in *The Village Voice* that the whites within the media were "promoting a gaggle of black female writers who pay lip service to the women's movement while supplying us with new stereotypes of black men and women." The word went out: white males were using black women as a backlash against the black male's dynamic assertion of manhood during the 1960s. Rumors sizzled: one of the more popular rumors was that some white woman at *Ms.* had actually written Wallace's book, *Black Macho and the Myth of the Super Woman*.

The upshot of the Shange and Wallace affair—which had been generalized to include not only women writers but intellectuals and activists as well—eventuated in the 1979 May/June issue of the *Black Scholar*. The issue was designated as: "The Black Sexism Debate."

There were seventeen writers and intellectuals in the issue: Ron Karenga, Robert Staples, Askia Toure, Harry Edwards, Audre Lorde, June Jordan, Ntosake Shange, Alvin Poussaint, Kalamu ya Salaam, Julianne Malveaux, Sarah Fabio, and Pauline Stone were among them. The specific initiative for the "debate" issue had been a review of *Macho*, by Robert Staples—"The

Myth of Black Macho; A Response to Angry Black Feminists"—
in the previous issue of the *Scholar*.

In both issues of the *Scholar*, it was clear that the men were
the ones who were angry. They were also less honorable than
the women. The words in the title of Staples's review of Wallace's book were twisted and turned against the women. The
men claimed that the women had fallen prey to white feminist
propaganda. They said, black women, like white women, had
been duped into turning against their men. The most truculent
assertion was that the writings of black women were "divisive"
to the cohesion of the black community. The men said, black
women writers were aiding the white male-dominated, racist,
capitalist society in its historical oppression of black people.
Unanimous among the men was the view that instead of making
up lies and half-truths about black males, black women should
be about the all-important business of exposing and fighting
racism and capitalism; so that the successful struggle of black
men rising to their rightful position of power and dominance in
their families, their communities, and in America in general,
would be hastened.*

The resentful emotions black men feel toward black women
writers are due to four unprecedented eventuations. (1) Black
women writers are declaring their independence like never before. (2) Black women writers are gaining autonomous influence over other black women. (3) Black women writers are
causing their existence to be seen and felt in areas of American
society and culture which have been heretofore barred to them.
(4) Black women writers are at last wresting recognition from
the white literary powers-that-be.

The telling thing about the hostile attitude of black men toward black women writers is that they interpret the new thrust
of the women as being "counter productive" to the historical
goal of the Black Struggle. Revealingly, while black men have
achieved outstanding recognition throughout the history of
black writing, black women have not accused the men of collab-
orating with the enemy and setting back the progress of the

---

* A notable exception to male hostility against *Black Macho* was an endorsement by
Ishmael Reed praising the book as "a stunning achievement."

race. During the 1960s, any number of black male writers were lauded by whites as being: "brilliant," "one of the best cultural critics now writing," "a formidably analytical mind" writing about "the forces that are currently molding our national destiny." After the publication of *Soul on Ice,* black women did not go berserk denouncing Eldridge Cleaver as an unscholarly, overgeneralizing sensationalist, or as a rapist, hater and batterer of black women—all of which were and are true. Yet, when Gayl Jones, author of *Eva's Man* and *Corregidora,* or Alice Walker in *The Third Life of Grange Copeland* and *The Color Purple,* or Ann Schockley, author of *Loving Her*—when these and other writers depict the hateful attitudes and violent treatment of black men toward black women, the men accuse these women of being black men-haters, bulldykes and perverse lovers of white men and women.

Black men write a lot about the "castrating" black female, and feel righteous in doing so. But when black women write about the incest, rape and sexual violence committed by black men against black females of all ages in the family and in the black community at large, and when black women write that black men are castrators and oppressors of black women, black men accuse the women of sowing seeds of "division" in the black community; the women are accused of promoting animosities not only between the sexes in general but between males and females in the black family itself. In other words, when the women tell the truth about men and refuse to accept the blame for what men have done to them, the men get mad as hell. They get "hurt." They try to discredit and invalidate the women.

Black male writers, for example, band together and write about the comraderie, competition, cooperation and brotherhood of black men in the struggle for manhood. This is viewed as manly and fitting by the men. But when black women write about the conflicts, joys, problems and sisterhood of black women in their struggle for self-esteem, black men brand the women "feminist bitches."

During periods when black men writers are in vogue, they hang out with white males in monosexual bars and cocktail lounges. They party, they wheel and deal on the literary scenes. Quite a few of the black writer machos of the 1960s rubbed shoulders with Norman Mailer, Leonard Bernstein, Jean Genet, Marlon Brando, and others of the so-called white liberal revolutionary *chic*. But when a black woman writer is said to have been seen in an all-women's bar, or is rumored to be associating with Gloria Steinem or Adrienne Rich, or even Grace Paley—black men writers feel "threatened." They fear that a "conspiracy" is being concocted not just against black men writers, but against the entire black race.

Toward the women writers, there are feelings of envy, jealousy, resentment and paranoia on the part of the men. These feelings emanate from a deep, philosophical structure of assumptions, values and wishes that black men have toward themselves as the male sex *vis-à-vis* the female sex. That the male sex is the boss and the females are the helpers, is what black men subscribe to. Black men therefore believe and feel that they are primary and sacred, and women are secondary and profane. Black men back up their notion of supreme self-importance by claiming that they, not women, are the prime target of the white men's oppressive system. Of course, none of this is true. But black men wish it to be true. Through the mechanism of the self-fulfilling prophecy they seek to will it, and force it, into truth. In other words, the beliefs, feelings and wishes of the men carry the mandate of a moral imperative. While the men are not primary and righteous, they feel they *ought* to be. This way, black men have a philosophy of manhood that relegates women to the back burner, coming and going. Therefore, it is perceived as an offense for black women to struggle on their own, let alone achieve something of their own. Such are the mortar and bricks out of which the mountain of sexism is constructed both before and on top of black women.

Hence, no matter how original, beautiful and formidable the works of black women writers might be, if such works bear the slightest criticism of black men, and if the women receive recognition from other women and especially from the white literary establishment—if such be the case, black men become "offended." They begrudge and resent the works and the authors too. They do not behave as though something of value has been added to the annals of black literature. Rather, they behave as though something has been subtracted from not only the literature but from the entire race. Specifically, men feel that something has been taken away from *them*. One of the most galvanizing examples of this is the disposition black men have toward Toni Morrison.

Morrison has won many prizes and awards. She sits in chairs of mainstream American literary organizations and is often the main speaker at major literary gatherings. Former senior editor at Random House, she has published four highly acclaimed novels, *The Bluest Eye, Sula, Song of Solomon,* and to date, *Tar Baby.* In 1981, articles about Morrison appeared in *New Republic, Essence, Nation, Soho News, Times* Book Review, *Vogue,* and other publications, culminating in the March 30 issue of *Newsweek,* on the cover of which appeared Morrison's photograph. Similar to several other contemporary black women writers, Toni Morrison is among the foremost Afro-American writers of all times. Since she was the first black woman to achieve this kind of status, one would think that black men would be proud of her accomplishments. On the contrary, I have witnessed black men, intellectuals, professors and writers alike, express resentments against Morrison ranging from the profound to the most petty. Variously she has been accused of "selling out," of turning back the clock of racial progress, of being a tool of white feminism, of being a black-man-hater, and engendering sexual immorality among black women.

[3]

Meanwhile, there are black women writers, poets, novelists, dramatists, critics, scholars, researchers, intellectuals, politicos and ideologues—hard at work. They are wielding their pens like spades unearthing forbidden treasures buried in old soil. They are bringing forth rough new uncut literary jewels of their lives, in which are reflected for the first time the truer wages of our history and our conduct. It is an adventurous literature and scholarship. There are both traditional and pioneer women writers, professed feminists and nonfeminists, and those who refuse to accept any label at all. Collectively, it is the *mass presence* of literature written by black women that is unprecedented.

In the past one had to search for black women-authored literature. Today the literature seeks you out.

Similar to women's writings in general, writings by black women enjoy a large audience. The audience comprises a heterogeneous readership of both blacks and whites, women and men. It is a popular audience. The works of Toni Morrison, Alice Walker, June Jordan, Toni Cade Bambara, Maya Angelou, Margaret Walker, Ntosake Shange, along with some newly recognized writers such as Octavia Butler (science fiction), Merita Golden and Mildred Taylor (novelists)—usually appeal to the popular female writer's audience.

There is, on the other hand, a readership within the popular audience which can be delineated as subpopular. Barbara Smith, Audre Lorde, Ann Shockley, Pat Parker, Donna Kate Rushin, Gloria T. Hull, Lorraine Bethel, Cheryl Clarke—and other lesbian feminist authors—are read more often than not by a subpopular audience of conscientious feminist black and white women, and a few men. While the writers appealing to the wider popular audience may or may not be lesbian feminists or feminists of any sort, the writers appealing to the subpopular readership are nearly all declared feminist women. Their works most often appear in limited circulating publications.

But the line between popular and subpopular readership—and between lesbian feminists, feminists, and non-declared feminists—is very thin. Just as the declared lesbian feminist writers are a part of the general pool of black women writers, so too is the subpopular audience a part of the larger readership. In other words, the people who read the works of lesbian feminist authors also read works of black women writers in general. The people who read black women writers in general, however, do not necessarily read the explicitly lesbian feminist writings. Depending on the subject and treatment of a particular piece of writing, a writer may be read by the popular audience, including the conscientious feminist readers. In another instance the readership for the same author may comprise only that portion of the general audience that is consciously involved with feminist issues. Many writers appeal to a "universal" audience. Alice Walker and Toni Morrison, for example, are usually read by both feminist readers as well as by non-feminist readers. Occasionally, a writer may "cross over." In 1984, Mary Helen Washington, a declared feminist writer, published an article, dealing with television images of black performers, in the national *TV Guide,* which is read by millions of television viewers.

It is noticeably on the part of declared black lesbian feminist writers that a black feminist criticism is being pioneered. This is not to take away from the other writers. All of the writers are blazing new trails. But especially the declared feminists and lesbian feminists—Barbara Christian, Mary Helen Washington, Barbara Smith, Ann Shockley, Cheryl Clarke, Wilmette Brown, and the rest—are in the forefront of the new critics, scholars, intellectuals and ideologues of our times.

But let us return to the sexual mountain. What is historically distinct about the present state of black writing in America is where it is coming from and where it seems to be inexorably going.

[4]

In 1937, in *Challenge* magazine, Richard Wright published an essay, "Blueprint for Negro Literature." The essay was reprinted in 1971 in *Amistad # II.* Wright asserted that a Marxist black male-oriented aesthetic and politic against racism and capitalism should be the all-consuming perspective of the Negro writer. Accordingly, the central character in all the Wright novels and stories is a young black male ensnared in the nightmare of a white racist capitalistic world. Wright was the first black writer to incorporate Marxism in a formulated black male aesthetic statement. But the masculine perspective itself, concerning the manhood of the black race, has always occupied center stage in the drama of Afro-American literature.

Along with its male-centered aesthetic, it is the hegemony of the masculine perspective that is now being changed—in and through the writings of black American women. In 1903, Dubois pointed out that the Negro, being both Black and American, shoulders a double consciousness. Black women have contended with the mountain of racism in America. But being at once Black, American, and Female, they have been victimized by the mountain of sexism, not only from the white world but from the men of the black world as well. Black women are bearers of what Barbara Smith calls, "geometric oppression." They are therefore bearers of a triple consciousness. To take but one of many examples, the perspective in the works of Alice Walker *(The Third Life of Grange Copeland, Meridian, In Love and Trouble, The Color Purple,* et cetera) is consistently informed with this consciousness. Since, however, the white feminist movement is ridden with racism, and since black men have tabooed and invested the word "feminism" with negative stigmata, many black women avoid calling themselves *feminists.* Alice Walker says she is a "womanist."

Whether you and I like it or not, both on the subpopular and popular levels the *de facto* situation is that a black feminist perspective pervades contemporary Afro-American literature. The perspective governs the aesthetic. The aesthetic informs the landscape and the vision. The literature, moreover, marks a significant juncture in the character of relations between black male writers and black female writers. For the first time, the status of black women writers is no longer relegated below the status of the males. Black women writers are taking the initiative. Instead of being constrained by and secondary to the literary dominance of black males, the literature of the women is expansive and liberating. Unlike in the past when women were supposed to be seen but not heard, the women of today are recognized writers in all fields and genres. Most importantly, black women are dealing with the sexual beliefs, feelings and actions that black men have maintained toward black females, in the street, in the family, and in the bedroom. They are dealing with the political machinations of these sexual beliefs and practices. Their perspective is faithful to the actual experiences of black women in America.

Consistent with the perspective is the aesthetic. Rather than a woman-to-man approach, it is a woman-to-woman approach. It is a black feminist aesthetic in which the form, language, syntax, sequence and metaphoric rendering of experience are markedly different and expansive in comparison to the male-authored literature. This can be witnessed in the works of Toni Morrison, especially in her *Bluest Eye,* and in Toni Cade Bambara's *The Salt*

Eaters, and Alice Walker's *Meridian,* and Gloria Naylor's *The Women of Brewster Place.*

The women are also engaged in research and scholarship. Works of black women long ignored are now being sought out and acclaimed. Having been castigated and dismissed as not being a "black" poet, particularly during the Black Power Era of the 1960s, Phillis Wheatley is being re-appraised by the women of today. Though she did not write much out of a black consciousness of slavery, Wheatley's works are imbued with a sensitivity that is specifically female. Similarly, works of Zora Neale Hurston, Dorothy West, Paule Marshall and Rosa Guy are being republished and seriously assessed for the first time. In the Winter 1980 issue of *Black American Literature Forum,* Margaret B. McDowell, Claudia Tate and Janet E. Sims published materials devoted to works of Ann Petry, Nella Larsen and Jessie Fauset. The American Women Writers Series of Rutgers University Press has republished Larsen's *Quicksand* and *Passing,* edited with an introduction by Deborah E. Mc-Dowell. Jean Carey Bond edited the Fourth Quarter 1979 issue of *Freedomways,* devoted to Lorraine Hansberry. In 1986 Ann Petry's much maligned novel, *The Street,* was finally reprinted. There is also new material coming out on Anne Spencer. "The Heart of a Woman," by Harlem Renaissance poet Georgia Douglas Johnson, is another example of the buried treasures that are being unearthed. Black women of heroic deeds are also being raised from behind the mountain of sexism—Anna Julia Cooper, Maria Stewart, Mary Terrell, Mary Bethune, Ida Wells, to mention a few.

Equally significant are the scholarly, expository and visionary writings. In the past, it was the men who wrote the sociology, history, political tracts, expository essays and ideological treaties. The traditional authorities on black women were overwhelmingly black males; they were the Duboises, Fraziers, Bennetts, Staples, Poussaints and Hares. As already cited, a black scholar was automatically assumed to be a black male. Even white women were more likely to be scholars on black women than black women were.

Today all of this is changing. Black women are scholars on themselves and on black men as well. There are the works of

Joyce Ladiner, Doris Y. Wilkinson, Carlene Young, Angela Davis, Lee Rainwater, Jean Carey Bond, Sharon Harley, Rosalyn Terborg-Penn, Paula Giddings, Johnnella Butler, Mary Helen Washington, Eleanor Traylor and many others. Edited by Gloria T. Hull, Patricia Bell Scott and Barbara Smith, the book, *But Some of Us Are Brave,* marks a primal attempt toward demystifying the traditional male-oriented sociology on black women and men, and is sent forth as a blueprint for a Black Women Studies curriculum. Founded in 1983, the magazine *SAGE: A Scholarly Journal on Black Women,* located in Atlanta, is consistently publishing literary and scholarly material on and by black women that is of the highest necessity and impeccable quality, edited by Patricia Bell Scott, Beverly Guy-Shjeftall, Jacqueline Jones Royster and Janet Sims-Wood. One of the hottest moments that transpired during the 1982 Black Studies Conference in Chicago was when black women advanced the resolution that, since Black Studies were decidedly Black Male Studies, Black Women Studies should be legitimized as an autonomous discipline. The women called for a plan of mutual cooperation between Black Studies and Black Women Studies.

What we are witnessing is an entire movement on the part of contemporary black women in general, and not just on the part of the so-called creative writers. Many of the women are Renaissance women, multiple in talent and endeavors, at once poets, novelists, mothers, scholars, workers, professors, intellectuals, and activists. Their efforts at the typewriter and in the world are toward reshaping the way we view the past, live in the present, and how we socialize our children for the future. When a child picks up a book called *Civil Wars,* by June Jordan, it is hoped that that child will encounter something more thorough of the Black Experience, in addition to what she or he will encounter in, say, a book by James Baldwin or Calvin Hernton. Because *Civil Wars* demonstrates that black women live generically in the world and relate generically to all things in the world. Just like any black man does.

Traditionally, we have been unaccustomed to books of sociocultural and political analysis authored by black women from a black feminist, or womanist, perspective. The race has had innumerable spokesmen. But never any spokeswomen. In their ambitious anthology, *Black Writers of America*, Barksdale and Kinnamon designate a section in the contents for "Racial Spokesmen"—Martin Luther King, Malcolm X and Eldridge Cleaver. No women are included. Since the unspoken and spoken assumption has been that the black race is a race of men, black women have had to specify their own existence, as represented by some of the titles of their books, Mari Evans's *I Am A Black Woman*, Sonia Sanchez's *I've Been A Black Woman*.

More and more women are assuming the task of being spokeswomen of black people, and writing socio-cultural-political essays and books. Hattie Gossett has completed a formidable work of this nature, seeking publication. Paula Giddings has published *When and Where I Enter*. The 1979 issue of CONDITIONS: FIVE, contains some thirty-odd women poets and writers. Edited by Lorraine Bethel and Barbara Smith, the issue represents some of the best of the new writings on realities black women and men live with every day, but which few of us have dared to write about before. Elaine Brown, ten years of high rank in the Black Panther Party, is searching for a publisher, and Shirley Ann Williams and Terry MacMillan have published widely received new novels, *Dessa Rose* and *Mama*, respectively.

It is significantly the conscientious feminists who are the most autonomous in their thinking and writing. They are the most challenging, and are forging unprecedented breakthroughs.

Black women are now emerging as foremost critics of our literature and our lives. Barbara Smith's "Towards a Black Feminist Criticism," and Deborah E. McDowell's "New Directions for Black Feminist Criticism," are primal efforts in building the new criticism and aesthetics. In her *Black Women Novelists: The Development of a Tradition, 1892–1976*, and her *Black Feminist Criticism: Perspective on Black Women Writers*, Barbara Christian exhibits painstaking analysis and cogent perceptions of a black womanist perspective in illuminating the works of Frances Ellen Watkins Harper, Paule Marshall, Toni Morrison, Alice Walker, Gwendolyn Brooks, Audre Lorde, and others. Margaret Walker is readying a work on Richard Wright, *The Deamonic Genius of Richard Wright*.

An integral part of what black women are doing consists of

bringing to the forefront what has been extant all along: That there is a humanity of black women and a world in their writings that have been historically, systematically overshadowed by the sexual mountain. In the July 1981 issue of *Essence*, Alexis De Veaux expressed the task of today's black women as follows:

> A struggle to express ourselves. To be heard. To be seen. In our own image. To construct the words. To name the deeds. Confront the risks. Write the history. Document it on radio, television and satellites. To analyze and live it.

Because much of the writing of contemporary black women is critical of black men, both in the literary sphere and in real life, the men find it unpalatable. But black writing owes its very nature to the oppressive conditions under which blacks were and are subjected in America. The function therefore of black literature has always been, as Langston Hughes so declared, to illuminate and elevate the condition of black people. It is altogether consistent with the heritage of black writing that black women write about the meanness they have experienced and still experience at the hands of black men as well as white men. It is inescapable that women writers seek to illuminate and elevate the condition of black women, their whole condition. How is one to participate meaningfully in the struggle between the races if one is the victim of subjugation within the race? In her 1925 *Survey Graphic* article, "The Double Task," Elise Johnson McDougald stated:

> In matters of sex equality, Negro women have contributed few outstanding militants. Their feminist efforts have been directed chiefly toward the realization of the equality of the races, the sex struggle assuming a subordinate place.

Today black women writers are challenging racism *and* sexism in all spheres of life and culture. Women having no avowed trek with feminism are increasingly engaged in literary activities that nevertheless fall within the scope of contemporary black womanist consciousness. Assisted by Margaret Porter of the *New York Times*, the New Bones group of New York women have sponsored literary affairs at Small's Paradise involving poets Lucille Clifton, Brenda Connor-Bey, Anasa Jordan, Geraldine Wilson and others. The book, *Black Women Writers at Work,* edited by Claudia Tate, contains conversation-interviews of fourteen outstanding black women writers. *Home Girls: A Black Feminist Anthology,* edited by the indefatigable Barbara Smith, contains some of the most woman-oriented black writers of today. Mari Evan and Erlene Stetson have also published critical anthologies. Forthcoming from Rutgers University Press is *The Tie That Binds: Political and Cultural Imperatives in the Renaissance of Afra-American Writings,* edited by Joanne Braxton and Andrea N. McLaughlin, and promises to be a comprehensive, water-breaking collection.

The scaling of the historic mountain of sexism on the part of contemporary black women writers does not mean that there are no differences or controversy between them. It certainly does not mean that their works are flawless and perfect. Some of their assertions are downright bombastic, some of their scholarship is questionable, and some of their quotations are very biased and misleading. Rather, the prolific propagation of literature by black women means that the sexual mountain need not remain as a barrier behind which black women writers must perish forever. There is much work to be done. The mountain must not merely be scaled, it must be destroyed.

Harsh sanctions on the part of black males exist against black feminism itself. There are even harsher sanctions against joint feminist efforts between black and white women. But, while combating racism within the white women's movement, more and more black women are accepting genuine cooperation from white feminists. Edited by Gloria I. Joseph and Jill Lewis, *Common Differences: Conflicts in Black and White Feminist Perspectives,* is an example of black and white women's efforts to iron out their problems. It is through the women's presses—*Essence, Ms., Off Our Backs, Heresies, Kitchen Table Press, Sage,* and so forth——that many black women are combating the sexist mountain. The Combahee River Collective in Boston is a group of dedicated black feminists who dominated the hallmark black women's issue of CONDITIONS: FIVE. As editor of The Feminist Press, Florence Howe has been responsive to the needs of black women by publishing and republishing black women's works of yesterday and today that have been obscured by the sexual mountain. It is, moreover, not in the established media but in black magazines and periodicals and noticeably in white feminist media that black women are accorded the all-important acknowledgment of having their writings seriously reviewed.

The present innovations in Afro-American literature are not isolated. They are part and parcel of the expanding consciousness of subjugated women all over the planet, particularly in "darkest" Africa. Black feminist writers are therefore engaged in a literature of demystification and liberation on a global scale. An examination of the perspective and landscape of the global literature of women of color reflects the same two tasks of which Elise McDougald spoke in 1925: (1) The demystification *illumination* of white male and female racism and imperialism over dark people, and (2) The specific liberation *elevation* of women of color from the fetters of both white and black male supremacy. For the last ten years the poetical works of Jayne Cortez constitute a one-woman arsenal of these two tasks.

The globalization of the Two Tasks is fostering alliances and cooperative literary efforts between Afro-American Women and women of the so-called Third World. In her article already noted, Alexis De Veaux writes:

> But like the women of Algeria, Cuba and Vietnam . . . Zimbabwean women often find themselves alienated from the society they helped liberate. In the so-called Third World it is a familiar pattern . . . the constraints of roles based on sex. . . . Black women in America and African Women in Zimbabwe . . . share the need for news of other women/cultures; the need to be active, and creative . . . we shake hands. We hug. We stretch the distance. . . .

The book, *This Bridge Called My Back: Writings by Radical Women of Color*, edited by Cherrie Moraga and Gloria Anzuldua, with a foreword by Toni Cade Bambara, contains prose, poetry, personal narratives and social analyses by Afro-American, Asian-American, Latina and Native American women. It is one of the many cooperative efforts reflecting an expanding "melting pot" of women's consciousness.

The works of Latin and African women writers in particular are now being brought to the foreground of black feminist consciousness. *Maru* and *A Question of Power*, by Bessie Head of South Africa; *Efuru*, by Flora Nwapa of Ghana; *No Sweetness Here*, by Christina Ama Ata Aidoo of Nigeria; *Three Solid Stones*, by Martha Mvengi of Tanzania; plus the scholarly work by Christina Abbo, *African Women: The Struggle for Economic Independence;* and the collectively edited work by Latin American Women, *Slaves of Slaves: The Challenge of Latin American Women*— these and other African, Latin and Third World publications are having an impact upon black women writers and Black Women Studies in the United States. Of course, the most widely read woman-identified African writer of today is the Nigerian born Buchi Emecheta, who has published five novels in rapid succession: *In The Ditch, The Bride Price, Second Class Citizen, The Slave Girl,* and *The Joys of Motherhood.*

We have always heard about the brotherhood of man. Now for the first time we are witnessing a literature the pervasive aesthetic of which is the sisterhood of women. In *Civil Wars,* June Jordan has written:

> I am a feminist, and what that means to me is . . . that I must undertake to love myself and to respect myself as though my very life depends upon self-love and self-respect . . . and that I am entering my soul into a struggle that will most certainly transform the experience of all the peoples of the earth, as no other movement can, in fact, hope to claim: because the movement into self-love, self-respect, and self-determination is the movement now galvanizing the true, the unarguable majority of human beings everywhere.

The literature of contemporary black women writers is a dialectical composite of what is known coming out of the unknown. It is an upheavel in form, style and landscape. It is the negation of the negative. And it proffers a vision of unfettered human possibility.

THREE

The Significance of Ann Petry

THE FEAR OF BIGGER THOMAS AND THE RAGE OF LUTIE JOHNSON

In 1946, with the publication of *The Street*, Ann Petry made a very special contribution to the tradition of black literature. Her novel includes all of the themes of protest historically associated with black writing. But the novel goes beyond these themes and is a milestone in the development of black writing because of its import for the specific tradition of black women writers. In one sweep, *The Street* captures the essence of the literature written by black women in the past while it brings to light the issues of the literature proliferated by today's black women. Moreover, in 1946, Petry made the boldest stroke that a black woman author had ever dared. *The Street* was the first writing in which a black man is killed by a black woman for being an unmitigated villain in the oppression of that woman.

It should be repeatedly emphasized that black women have always cried out against injustice. The first American-born woman to speak in public was black. In the early 1800s in Boston, Maria Stewart rallied in defense of her black sisters. "Oh,

Ye Daughters of Africa!" she called to them. Although Stewart spoke and wrote for the uplifting of both women and men, she was jeered by the men because she was a female. Pleadingly she cried out to the men, "What If I Am a Woman!" Again, in 1827, in the first newspaper owned by black men *(Freedom's Journal)*, Stewart sent in a letter under a pseudonym, "Matilda," pleading with the men to include specifically black women in the uplifting of the race. During the heyday of the anti-slavery and women's rights struggles, another voice, Sojourner Truth, cried out to the world, "Ain't I a Woman!" Then when the men were pursuing their newly won freedom, another black woman, Anna Julia Cooper, pleaded the question of "When and Where" would black women enter. All during the 1800s and well into the twentieth century black women writers, poets, and novelists, continued to plea for the humanity of black women. It should be noted also that Frank J. Webb, W. E. B. Dubois, Benjamin Brawley, Wallace Thruman, and especially Jean Toomer and Langston Hughes, along with other early black men writers, had also written of the hardships and virtues of black women. But no one until Petry, male or female, had so thoroughly portrayed black women as victims of Multiple Oppression, and no one had so boldly portrayed black men as the levelers of a significant measure of that oppression.

The Street marked the juncture between the restraining colorations of nineteenth-century Victorian "colored lady's" writings (as in Frances Harper's *Iola LeRoy,* 1892, and even later in Gwendolyn Brooks's *Maude Martha,* 1953) and the forging of a proletarian black woman's fiction. Since the first wave of black migration out of the South shortly after the demise of Reconstruction, black women had been coming to the northern cities. But there had simply been no serious treatment of black underclass women, neither in the narratives and early novels, nor in the "primitivist" and "tragic mulatto" portrayals of Harlem Renaissance writers, such as Claude MacKay and Nella Larsen or Jessie Fauset. Although Janie in Hurston's *Their Eyes Were Watching God* (1937) was a breakaway from the restraining Victorian portrayal of black women, and despite Dorothy West's Cleo Judson in *The Living Is Easy* (1946), until Petry there had been no such women as Lutie Johnson, Min, and Mrs. Hedges in the entire history of black fiction. No one had made a thesis of the debilitating mores of economic, racial and sexual violence let loose against black women in their new urban ghetto environment. In both texture and substance, *The Street* is the first work of social realism and naturalism written from an all but complete Womanist Perspective.

[2]

Similarly, what Petry achieved for the history and future of black women's literature, the 1940 publication of *Native Son* by Richard Wright achieved the same thing for black men's literature. Wright and Petry had been preceded by a whirlwind cultural movement in the 1920s which was dubbed the New Negro/Harlem Renaissance. The first movement of its kind, the Renaissance writers vigorously debated the age-old issue of how should Negroes be portrayed in works of art. As already mentioned, Dubois and Langston Hughes published manifesto articles—"Criteria for Negro Art" and "The Negro Artist and The Racial Mountain"—in which they respectively set forth their views of what amounted to a "Black Aesthetic" for the first time in the annals of black writing.* Again, a decade later, in 1937, a third black aesthetic manifesto—"Blueprint for Negro Literature"—was published in *Challenge* magazine (later *New Challenge*) by Richard Wright. Black male writers during the 1930s, such as Langston Hughes, Roi Ottley, Walter White, and others, as well as those before and after them, were always concerned about, in the words of Langston Hughes, the "elevation and illumination of the Negro people." In his article, however, Wright incorporated the unprecedented assertion that a Marxist philosophy should be the ruling principle in the treatment of the Negro situation in America. Thus, in 1940, *Native Son* became the first black social realist-naturalist novel to depict consciously the sundry effects of racism and capitalism on black males in the American urban ghetto environment. Highlighting the black family, and connecting the political with the personal,

* For Dubois's article see *Crisis.* Vol. 32, No. 6 (October 1926). For Hughes's, see *Nation.* June 23, 1926.

the novel decisively emphasizes the plight of black male youth in a torrential masculine landscape in which the protagonist, Bigger Thomas, murders two women, one white and one black.

In addition to similarities in genre (social realism and naturalism), there are other apparent similarities between *Native Son* and *The Street*. The protagonists of both novels, Bigger Thomas and Lutie Johnson, are young American-born blacks living in ghetto areas of two sprawling urban cities, Bigger on the South Side of Chicago, and Lutie on 116th Street, Harlem, New York. Both are conscious of being hated and oppressed by white society. Both share a sense of fear and are haunted by feelings of guilt. Lutie is estranged from her family and loved ones; although Bigger lives with his family, a brother, sister, and mother, there is no understanding between them and their relations are strained by distance and coldness. Both Bigger and Lutie are ambitious. Though he knows not what, Bigger yearns to be "something." Although Lutie is sure of what she wants out of life, she, like Bigger, feels trapped, thwarted, is nagged by an underlying sense of impending doom. In all of this they seem to be kindred spirits.

Although the situations of Bigger and Lutie appear to be the same, and while the similarities may be real enough, a closer look reveals that the qualitative, substantive aspects of Lutie's and Bigger's conditions are miles apart. There is no familyness among members of Bigger's family, nevertheless Bigger is living in the house with his family, and he has never been married. Lutie, on the other hand, has been married and is now estranged from her husband as well as from her parents. She is a "single parent" living in a cramped room in a run-down building with her young son. While Bigger has his gang cronies and a girlfriend, Bessie, Lutie is completely alone, with no friends of either sex. Lutie murders one person, a black man who has persistently offended her and who attempts to rape her. She murders him in an explosion of rage without aforethought. Bigger, on the other hand, murders two women out of "instinctive" fear—one, a white woman, "accidentally"; the other, his girlfriend, he murders with calculated brutality after having raped her, because he perceived her as a liability to his safety.

For all of Wright's Marxist analysis, *Native Son* is at heart a psychological novel. Wright was possessed by a driving pursuit of the effects of oppression on the psychology of its victims. Although the novel is written in the third-person narrative, and though the Chicago landscape blanketed with the whiteness of snow is ever present, it is Bigger, and Bigger alone, who dominates the novel. Or, rather, it is Richard Wright himself who dominates every page of the gruesome tale.

It was this way with almost everything Wright wrote, the sheer power of his imposing narrative always makes you know it is Wright writing and talking to you. The much criticized Marxist analytical summation speech of Bigger's lawyer, Max, is nobody but Richard Wright expounding.

The Street, by contrast, is written in the third person in earnest. So earnest, in fact, that frequently the third person narrative easily translates into the first person. Petry sets Lutie loose on her own: I see what Lutie sees, I feel her feelings, I experience her being, I get angry with her for her blindnesses and for having emotions and beliefs with which I disagree. The same applies to the other characters, both the major and minor ones as well. They exist independently of Ann Petry. Likewise, so does the world in which the characters grapple with the forces of existence; without any effort on our part, we experience the milieu of 116th Street and the surrounding white world as living organisms in themselves.

The Street, moreover, deals with not just one dominating character, but with lots of people. In addition to Lutie Johnson, Min, and Mrs. Hedges, there are in-depth portrayals of Boots Smith and William Jones (the "Super"), and the white man, Junto. There are a host of other "minor" characters both black and white, including Lutie's husband and family and, of course, her son, Bud. There are the ever-present women, men, and children of 116th Street, the young girls, the older "bag ladies," and the eternal "domestics" of all work. We experience the changing of the seasons along with the moods and countenances of the *black masses* hanging out on corners, on stoops, and in the joints, hustling, fighting, laughing, drinking, trudging along, existing and being. *The Street*, the novel, becomes more than a work of art. It is a living, organic life, utterly real and altogether natural.

In *Native Son,* none of this is portrayed. There is only Bigger, only Wright, dominating the scene. Despite the singular power of Wright's heady prose, *Native Son* is far from being comparable to the richness of *The Street.*

Yet the publication of *Native Son* established Richard Wright as the patriarch of black writing. He, of course, had his detractors. But Wright's greatness as the first revolutionary black man writer is unquestionable. During his lifetime, he was accorded worldwide recognition and achieved immortal fame.

By comparison, Petry has received only a meager amount of acclaim, and that was short-lived. Lots of people thought *The Street* was a "carbon copy" of *Native Son* (which was also said of *Knock on Any Door,* by Willard Motley). The great white critic of black fiction, Robert Bone, wrote—*incredibly!*—that Petry's novel offered a "superficial analysis of life in the ghetto." Petry was judged as just another one of those Negro women writers. Only recently has her contribution begun to receive adequate evaluation, and solely on the part of black women literary purveyors. In her Ph.D. thesis, *The Ironic Vision of Four Black Women Novelists,* Beatrice Royster included *The Street* as an example of an immortal, visionary piece of writing. Gloria Wade-Gayles devoted about fifteen cogent pages to *The Street* in her water-breaking literary work, *No Crystal Stair: Visions of Race and Sex in Black Women's Fiction.*

Let's face it. *Native Son* is an astounding Patriarchal achievement. In its pages Richard Wright is exclusively concerned with the denial of Manhood to black American youth and the resulting demise of psychological health of inner-city black men. Nothing at all is said about the womenfolk. The fact of a singular dominance in *Native Son* is sufficiently indicative of the novel's overriding phallic perspective. In the room, as Bigger smothers to death the limp drunken white woman, and in the abandoned tenement building, as he actually rapes and slaughters his black girlfriend, he experiences a violent inner passion that is orgasmic.

In a revised version of his "Blueprint" manifesto, Wright acknowledged the Triple Oppression of black women.* He also

* See *Amistad #1.* John A. Williams, Charles Harris (eds.), Vintage Books, Random House, 1970.

depicted black male sexism in various later works, such as, for example, in the posthumously published novel *Lawd Today.* Wright, moreover, held in great esteem the writings of Gertrude Stein and formed a mentor-type friendship with her. Nevertheless, he never got around to treating or portraying black women in his work from a woman's perspective. Again, this is not to take away from Wright. Wright, along with John A. Williams and Chester Himes, is among the world's greatest socially committed male-oriented writers.

[3]

In *The Street,* however, Petry's concern richly varies over a wide range of people and sensibilities. Most of all, she treats black women as both black *and* female, and, in addition to racism and capitalism, Petry incorporates the third dimension in black women's lives—sexism. *The Street* is a pioneer Womanist Feminist novel, depicting the nature of Geometric Oppression that is imposed on black women from both without and within the black race. To refer to this oppression as simply "triple"— merely to add up in an arithmetic way the effects of capitalism, racism, and sexism—does not begin to calculate the Terribleness of *Geometric* Oppression. The diagram shown will help to illuminate the multiple machinations of geometric oppression in *The Street.*

On all sides Lutie Johnson is trapped by the big three *isms* of American white and black societies. At the top is Capitalism, represented and personified in the novel by the Chandlers, for whom Lutie works as a "domestic." The Chandlers (both the men and the women) are also racist and sexist toward Lutie. Wealthy and decadent, they are in possession of the American Dream, they have all the "finer things" of the American way. Below the Chandlers is Junto, a misfit white man who owns property and joints in the black ghetto, along with other such enterprises elsewhere. He is a parasitic exploiter of the misery and poverty of the black community. He controls Mrs. Hedges, who lives in one of his run-down tenements, and who runs a whorehouse. On either side of the diagram are Racism and Sexism. To the left there is William Jones, the superintendent of the

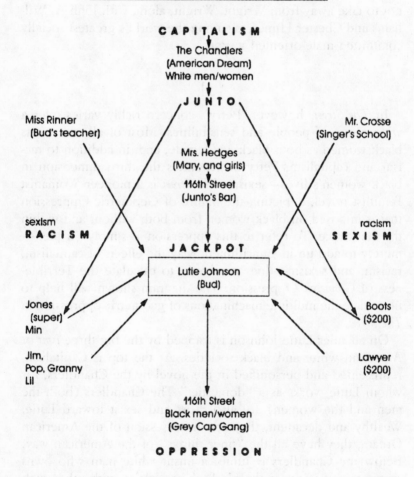

The Geometric Oppression of Lutie Johnson

CAPITALISM
The Chandlers
(American Dream)
White men/women

JUNTO

Miss Rinner
(Bud's teacher)

Mr. Crosse
(Singer's School)

Mrs. Hedges
(Mary, and girls)

116th Street
(Junto's Bar)

sexism
RACISM

racism
SEXISM

JACKPOT
Lutie Johnson
(Bud)

Jones
(super)
Min

Boots
($200)

Jim,
Pop, Granny
Lil

Lawyer
($200)

116th Street
Black men/women
(Grey Cap Gang)

OPPRESSION

building in which both Lutie and Mrs. Hedges live. Beneath Jones is Min, the battered girl-woman he keeps and treats like he treats his dog. Still on the left are Jim, Lutie's husband, and Pop, Granny, and Lil, members of her family household. There is a lawyer on the right, a minor character who is nevertheless significant in Lutie's terribleness.

Down the center are Junto's Bar and the men, women, girls, and boys of 116th Street. On the right is Boots Smith, another one of Juno's ghetto puppets. On the left is Bud's white schoolteacher, Miss Rinner. Mr. Crosse is on the right, owner of a singer's school where Lutie seeks employment.

Lutie Johnson is in the center. She and her young son, Bud, are in the JACKPOT.

All of these people, in and through the machination of the big three *isms,* are gunning for Lutie Johnson, and keep her in an ever-mounting state of frustration and insecurity. The dimensions of Lutie's oppression are not one plus one plus one, but one time two times three times all the people and impersonal forces she encounters. The sheer weight of this oppression is indeed *terrible.*

[4]

Lutie's situation is that she has been married to Jim, and they have a son, Bud. Soon the family runs into trouble, Jim loses his job, cannot find another one, and Lutie has to work as a "domestic" requiring her to "live in," and can only visit her family once every two weeks. One day Lutie comes home unexpectedly and catches Jim with a woman. Jim is drunk, as he has taken to drinking since being unable to countenance his wife's working "outside the home." Lutie is hurt to the quick, a fight ensues, after which Lutie takes Bud and leaves the family. Short of money, she and Bud find a cubbyhole of a place in the heart of the ghetto on 116th Street. Alone, isolated, a "single parent," Lutie desperately seeks to find suitable employment and to raise her son in a decent manner. But everywhere she turns she runs head-on into people perceiving and behaving toward her as but a sex object. The superintendent of her building, William Jones, gets the "hots" for Lutie, constantly harasses her, and eventually attempts to rape her.

Mrs. Hedges' apartment is a whorehouse; she sits all day peering out of her window down on the street looking for prospective whores among the young girls newly arrived from down south. She perceives Lutie as a "prized catch" for her boss and friend, Junto, who owns the building and provides protection for Mrs. Hedges through his "connections" with the local cops.

Nobody perceives Lutie as she is, but merely as a potential whore; they *insist* on it. The rich white family, the Chandlers, for whom she is obliged to work as a "domestic," regard her as a workhorse and as a sexual threat to the female Chandlers, who believe all black women are promiscuous sluts ready to jump in bed with any and every white man. Lutie receives racist and sexist harassment from Mr. Crosse at his singer's school, where she answered an advertisement for prospective singers, and she is rebuffed by other white and black employment prospects all along the way. "A nice-looking girl like you . . . a nice-looking girl like you . . . should not have to worry about money . . . a nice-looking girl like you. . . ."

Growing grim, Lutie maintains her determination to "make it" in the world in a manner befitting a respectable colored woman with a young son, a son who by now is mystified by his mother's growing bitterness and her being away from home so much, and who fares poorly in school where his white teacher, Miss Rinner, hates the "smell" of her black pupils. Also, by now, Jones has become totally crazed over not having Lutie and begins to dog and batter Min, his live-in sex servicer, who in turn harbors feelings of resentment toward Lutie. "Everything was all right until *she* came," growls Min.

Tired and frustrated, one evening Lutie wanders into Junto's bar and grill on the corner of 116th Street. As when she walks along the street, in the bar she is instantly perceived as "ready meat." Boots Smith, the black henchman of Junto, spots Lutie and proceeds to "hit" on her. Boots "dates" her for an instant, rides her in his shiny pimp's car and, when rebuffed, offers her a singing job with a band he manages. Junto hears of this and persuades Boots to set a trap for Lutie. Junto wants her for himself.

Meanwhile, because of Jones, Bud has gotten arrested. Desperate, Lutie goes to a lawyer who does not inform her that she does not need a lawyer because Bud is under age and will no doubt be released on probation into Lutie's custody. Instead, the lawyer says his fee will be $200. Seeking to borrow the money from Boots (who is "rolling in dough") Lutie is lured to Boots's apartment on "Sugar Hill" under pretense of being lent the money. Here, finally, and fatally, Lutie strikes back.

[5]

All of this is portrayed in painstaking, graphic, naturalistic detail. *The Street* is populated with frustrated, twisted, deformed, victimized, beaten-down, impoverished people, a few of whom, such as Boots, Jones, and Mrs. Hedges, claw their way off the bottom of the heap and prey upon the rest. Mrs. Hedges is a "mountain" of a woman, and is utterly "unattractive." Down south, when she was young, she was trapped in a fire, suffering burns all over her body; her hair was burned away and she must wear a wig. Stubbornly embittered, she made her way north, to Harlem, where she roamed the streets pilfering garbage cans and living in doorways. One night she meets a white man in the same condition as she, an ugly, dumpy wretch, and they are drawn to each other. The man is Junto, who is also endowed with sheer stubbornness. Together they form a team, and start a junk business. The white man and the black woman are beyond racial prejudice and hate. But, observing the rules of society, Junto puts the money earned through his brains and Mrs. Hedges' labor to good use; he works his way up the ladder, acquires property and several bars and nightclubs in Harlem and other parts of Manhattan; he makes the necessary connections with the big boys downtown, and becomes a kingpin of a sort. He sets Mrs. Hedges up in the whoring business and provides protection. In turn, she is loyal to Junto and steers some of her "girls" his way.

Though she has money, an apartment, and "security" of a sort, all Mrs. Hedges ever really wanted in life is what she cannot have, "a man who will fall in love with her"! But she is "repulsive," with burn scars and no hair, Lord, *no hair!* So she sits framed in her window, with a bandanna around her head, casting eyes of prey down on the street in search of "girls" for her business. She calls everybody "dearie."

As soon as Mrs. Hedges sights Lutie she greets her, "dearie," and is convinced that the young, well-dressed, dignified newcomer is fit for her trade, or, better yet, for Junto who, she knows, wants to sleep with a nice, warm, colored girl. Though Mrs. Hedges shows some human kindness by stopping Jones from raping Lutie in the darkened hall and invites Lutie to tea, she is thinking all the while of "catching" Lutie for Junto. Mrs. Hedges is a vampire who puts the "girls" out of doors when they have earned no money. It requires much stamina of Lutie to keep from being sick in her presence.

Then there is Min, who fearfully believes in the decree which says, "A woman alone has no chance." The fear that she must have a man to protect her drives her from man to man. Thus, after the last man, Min "took up" with Jones. Though she is "protected" from other men, she is not protected from the incredible beastliness of the very man with whom she lives. Similar to nearly all underclass women, Min has been beaten down by facile forces of oppression on every side. In order to survive, she has succumbed and accommodated herself to nothing less than enslavement. She knows it is wrong, but she feels helpless against white people, women in particular, who work her like a mule of the world and slander her black sexuality, which makes her, we're told, more accepting and expecting of the battering she receives from the men in her life. More than one of the men she has lived with (for "protection") has pimped her, taken her money, used and abused her, stayed drunk, and then left her. In the dimly lit hovel of Jones's apartment, she exists as though she were a hostage. Silent, inarticulate, tipping about, she is forever trying to make herself invisible. She feels "ugly," she feels at fault, for what?—she does not know—for being a woman, surely. In her crampy room there is a caged canary and Min's table with crawfoot legs: these are Min's signs. She is utterly confined without friends, male or female. Jones treats her like he does his dog, whom he abuses whenever something irritates him.

But things were not as bad as they became after Lutie Johnson moved into the building and Jones became fixated with her. After his failure at raping Lutie, Jones becomes insanely cruel. He beats Min and hates her "ugliness," because he wants Lutie and cannot "get" her.

Similar to Albert in *The Color Purple*, who beats Celie because Celie is not Shug, the taking out of frustration on the woman in the house is standard traditional procedure. Men oppress, batter, and make women "ugly." Then men turn around and beat them some more for being "ugly." This is precisely what happens in Alice Walker's novel *The Third Life of Grange Copeland*. Significantly, Petry points out that all the men in Min's life have treated her as have her white employers, even worse.

But Min is a survivor. She has heard of a "root doctor," Prophet somebody or other, who can cure "nocturnal disappearances" of husbands and lovers.

Although Jones comes to have a constant urge to "kick her ass," Min obtains from the Prophet some conjure potion and a golden cross which she hangs over her bed, along with candles that she burns constantly. Held at bay by Min's newly acquired "mojo," Jones kicks the dog's ass instead. By now, though, Min has come to fear for her life. Jones, a "sick crazy animal," might kill her at any time. The sheer instinctive reflex for self-preservation signals her that it is time to run. Through all the torture that has been inflicted on her, Min has somehow held on to the belief that "a person has a right to live." She sneaks out, and takes up with a familiar pushcart man of the neighborhood. We know, and fear, what is going to happen here too. But Min survives for another day, at least.

[6]

While Min's life is her life, it is at the same time a representation of the lives of all the women in *The Street*. As Lutie walks up and down 116th Street, back and forth to her apartment, there are constant references to the women who populate the neighborhood. Lutie sees them, smells them, she hears their talk, their laughter, their complaints and wails. The young females and teenagers, catering to the attention of boys and men; the older and aged women sitting, standing, leaning against lamp-posts and buildings, moving along, burdened down from their "domestic" jobs, long ago deserted by their husbands, or shouldering the responsibilities of providing for their families, since their men cannot or will not find employment.

As she witnesses 116th Street, Lutie is fearfully haunted by the thought that she might end up like these women, broken, worn out before their time, and resigned bitterly to their fate. She rejects the feeling, determined to get away before it becomes too late. Lutie is aware of the buildings themselves: the hallways and rooms are like dungeons inside, the walls reach out for Lutie. The shops, stores, and groceries along the street are stuffed with expensive cheap clothing fit for one wearing only, and inferior food selling for the highest prices. "Burly Negro," headlines in the newspapers. Old black men "aimlessly staring." Gangs of boys. "Hey, fine momma! Hey, ugly bitch!" The homeless girls. Lutie sees and does not see Mrs. Hedges leaning eternally out of her window, bandanna-covered head, vulture eyes ever-watchful for a nice young "catch." As she mounts and descends the dreaded stairs to and from her apartment, Lutie sees whores and johns, boys and girls in the hallways, plying their trades and shortening their lives.

Cold, cheerless nights; hot, crowded days. The cursing in other people's apartments, the fighting. "Black bitch, I oughta kill you long ago!" The loud music on radios, the advertisements for "beauty" products. The church music, the smell of alcohol. No hope, no life. The bitter resignation, the crowded hospital every Saturday night, the blood spilled, the jobless men, the broken families, the desolation, the sense of loss, the white cops, always the white cops, and the poverty. Oh yes, the poverty! The lack of money, money, money.

Lutie is in any ghetto anywhere in America: Cleveland, Chicago, Detroit, Boston, Los Angeles, Washington, D.C. A quarter century will pass and Gwendolyn Brooks will pen the line "sick and influential," describing the stairs Lutie has to climb, and will again portray in great poetic language the draconian irony of the "Mecca" that Lutie is witnessing in 1946.

[7]

In 1965, two decades later, a renowned black social scientist, Kenneth Clark, would publish a book entitled *Dark Ghetto*, in which he would write:

> The dark ghetto's invisible walls have been erected by white society, by those who have power, both to confine those who have no power and to perpetuate their powerlessness. The dark ghettos are social, political, educational, and—above all—economic colonies. Their inhabitants are subject peoples, victims of the greed, cruelty, insensitivity, guilt, and fear of their masters. (*Dark Ghetto*, p. 11.)

Dark Ghetto is an authoritative study of black America, the first of its kind by a black social scientist. But when it comes to black women in the ghetto, the book is a failure. On pages 67–74, it even adheres to the viewpoint of black males' being unable, "due to slavery and lack of wherewithal," to "act out their *normal* desires for dominance" (my emphasis). The book also propagates the myth of "matriarchy" among black women, while it says nothing of value about the oppression and violence imposed on black women by black men.

Twenty years before the publication of Clark's book, *The Street* anticipated all that *Dark Ghetto* encompasses, and went beyond it to include the lives of more than half of the black population whom Clark chose to leave out of his most acclaimed work. When it comes to the beliefs, feelings, and behavior that are maintained by black men toward black women, Petry's novel is worth more than all the man-sociology ever written on the subject.

The Street does not philosophize, preach, or theorize. It depicts and portrays. It shows that the black ghetto is not only a social, political, educational, and economic colony, but that the black ghetto is also, and foremost, a *sexual* colony. If black people are little more than colonized slaves, then black women are multiple slaves. They are slaves of the white racist society, which exploits their labor and services while holding them at bay in the apartheid-like "homeland" ghettos; they are a "market," a reserve of slaves for white men who plunder and pillage them as sex objects in white homes and in "brothels" inside and outside of the ghettos; they are once more slaves of black men within the confines of the ghettos, in their homes and along the public streets. In this last instance, black women are slaves of slaves, they are "game" and "sport" for black men who harass them, hold them hostage, batter them, hate, demean, oppress them, repress them, pimp, exploit and kill them, and dare black women to regard this behavior as offensive, let alone make it public.

[8]

In *The Street,* Jones the super, and Boots the henchman of Junto, are archetypical paradigms of all the woman-hating sexism that black men at large and black society in general harbor toward and level against the women in their midst. Because of the political, economic, and social racism of white society and culture, Jones and Boots have "righteous excuses" to be all the more dehumanized and all the more monstrous toward the "opposite" sex, and toward Lutie in particular. But they are sexists anyway. Their specific experiences with the white world merely exacerbate their already deeply ingrained sexist dispositions.

Jones, for example, is depicted as a beast. His apartment is like the hold of a cargo ship, darkened and crowded with his junky stuff. We learn that he drove all the women out of his life by his violent sex. On the street, lounging in front of the building, he undresses women with his eyes, molests them in his mind. His feelings toward the women are about performing sexual harm on them, to prove how powerful and dominating he is. He hates the images he conjures up in his mind of Lutie and her husband having sex. Then he hates Lutie and "desires" her even more. To Jones, Lutie is a "piece of meat," an assemblage of body parts, a "thing" on which he can take out his hatred against the female sex, in and through the violence of "fucking."

In the opening scenes of the novel, when Lutie encounters him as she comes to apply for the apartment, I was unbelieving of Petry's description of Lutie's perception of Jones. We have been conditioned to deny the ugliness that men impose on women, and blame the women. "Men may not be angels but they are not as bad as women depict them," is what we are conditioned to say. Lutie's impressions of him must be "paranoia." She has just met the man. How can she think so badly of him? She thinks Jones's eyes are "hungry." As he follows her up the stairs to show her the apartment, Lutie observes that he has "a long black flashlight . . . the rod of its length . . . as black as his hand." She feels his presence as "menacing," and that Jones is lusting after her. I am thinking, as I read, that this middle-class-oriented woman thinks she is better than this old worn-down Negro man. She must be "color-prejudiced" against him because he is so black and she is a smooth brown. She must have some kind of Freudian complex as well.

But Lutie's impressions prove to be more than accurate. Obsessed and enraged, Jones enters her apartment when she is at work and ingratiates himself to Bud, who is there. While pretending to make repairs, he rambles through her personal things. When he is done, he can be heard gulping down beer and emitting orgasm sounds.

Jones is so certain that Lutie is nothing but a "whore," that when she wards off his repeated advances, he believes at first that she does not comprehend his intentions, he has not made himself clear enough. But after Lutie, along with Mrs. Hedges, fights off his rape attempt, Jones decides he knows the reason Lutie will have nothing to do with him. "She was in love with Junto, the white man. Black men weren't good enough for her. He had seen women like that before." He fantasizes about Lutie and "the white man" together in copulation; his anger almost kills him. He vows "revenge." He plots and succeeds at getting Bud into trouble.

[9]

Boots Smith is a younger version of Jones. He had been a down-and-out pianist during the Depression days, playing in low-class joints. He hated playing in those joints, with the drunken white people shouting "nigger" insults and giving "Hey, boy" commands. He finally landed a regular job as a

Pullman porter, and it was more of the same, "Hey, boy! Come 'mere, boy!" But it was better than playing in those joints, and he vowed he would never play the piano again. He got married to Jubilee. Then, upon returning from being on a Pullman run, he got a glimpse of a white man descending the fire escape leading from their apartment window. He had noticed the curtain blowing in the breeze as he entered the apartment. He beat Jubilee and would have killed her, but she ducked under his arm, grabbed a kitchen knife and sliced his face, leaving him scarred for life.

There had been lots of women since, but Boots could not remember them, except that he had kicked most of them around, always remembering the curtain blowing in the breeze. He ended up frequenting Junto's bar, which he liked because there was no racism in there. Even though he had sworn off the piano, on one occasion he sat down and began playing. A white man, Junto, came over and complimented him, and offered him a job as manager of the bar's fledgling band. There had not been any white-black bigotry from Junto, who was impressed with Boots's successful building of the band and rewarded Boots accordingly, such that by the time Lutie comes to the neighborhood Boots is able to "buy anything in the world he wanted."

Boots saw Lutie and wanted her. He saw her the way he saw Jubilee, and saw all women. He regarded her the same way Lutie's husband, Jim, regarded her and the same way that Jones felt toward all women. His lust for her was a lust for power over her, a lust to dominate and "revenge" himself for what white men had done to him, for surely they had robbed him of his manhood. Boots had been made to feel "less than a half man, because he didn't even have a woman of his own, because he not only had to say 'Yes, sir,' he had to stand by and take it while some white man grabbed off what belonged to him."

The curtain in the window began to blow in the breeze of Boots's mind. He offers to drive Lutie in his shiny pimp's car to her place of "domestic" employment. His attitude is blasé, pimpish, superior, mannish. Wheeling the car at accelerated speed through the city "made him feel he was a powerful being who could conquer the world. . . . It was like playing god."

On a single page Boots addresses Lutie as "baby" more than a half dozen times, he never calls Lutie by her name throughout the novel. When she replies that she is single, he guns the car forward and flippantly remarks, "Never saw a good-looking chick yet who didn't belong to somebody," as though it were against the law for a woman to belong to herself.

Boots is wearing suede gloves; Lutie observes him and knows that he considers her a "pick up." As he hurls the car through the night, she thinks that he is making up for a lot of the things that have happened to him to make him what he is, that he is "proving all kinds of things to himself." But she is so desperate for a better job, and he has offered to get her an audition with the band, that she decides to "play the game," thinking to pull out before the kill. She tells him the reason she broke up with her husband, and how Jim accused her of "other niggers" and beat her, "because the fact that he couldn't support his wife and child . . . undermined his belief in himself until he could no longer bear it. And he got himself a woman . . . his self-respect was momentarily restored through the woman's desire for him." After Lutie tells him this, Boots says to her, "You don't have to be poor any more. Not after tonight. I'll see to that. All you got to do from now is just be nice to me, baby."

But, fighting off his repeated advances, Lutie refuses to be "nice" to him. Plus, by now, Junto wants her and orders Boots hands-off and to string her along about the singing job with the band. He tells Boots to promise her but not to pay her; instead, he is to give her presents. "Women like to receive presents," says Junto, believing what men believe and foster on women to make them feel like grateful children rather than like grown women. To convince Boots that he means what he says, Junto issued him a warning, saying, "Whoever makes a man can also break him!" Boots considers the alternatives, but Lutie did not weigh enough against a lifetime slaving for and "uncle tomming" to white men.

On page 171, we find that Boots would sell out a hundred Lutie Johnsons, a hundred black women, to keep money in his pocket. Anyway, the urgency of his desire for Lutie was but an urgency that Petry portrays as being at the base of men's desire for women—to "conquer and subdue." Boots's attitude toward

Lutie is every man's attitude toward every woman, only now in the extreme. He exploits Lutie's desperation for the $200 lawyer's fee that the lawyer has misled her to believe she needs to get her son, Bud, out of police custody. Boots arranges an appointment at his apartment. The "appointment" is a deliberate set-up for Junto, who is to be there. Lutie arrives, Junto is hiding in a back room and overhears Lutie refusing to become his concubine. She is indignant, hurt, outraged. Junto slips out of the apartment. Boots says to him, "Don't worry, Mack. She'll come around. Come back about ten o'clock." Then:

> He closed the door quietly behind Junto. . . . He thought of the thin curtains blowing in the wind . . . this time a white man can have a black man's leavings. . . . This would be his revenge. . . . He reached out and slapped her . . . he slapped her again. "Maybe after I beat the hell out of you a coupla times, you'll begin to like the idea of sleeping with me and with Junto." (pp. 262–65.)

[10]

But Boots is mistaken. Lutie Johnson will not be compromised by him, or Junto, or by anybody or anything. From the very beginning, as the cold November wind violently assaults the world of the street, Lutie is presented with a certain dignity and strength of character. The wind mounts a ravishing attack but it fails to vanquish her. She braces her body against the wind and refuses to be blown about.

Throughout the novel, through all the debilitating things that happen to her, though shaken, Lutie is steadfast until the very end. Men, the street, and the world at large beat and batter her. But they do not conquer or subdue her.

On the other hand, Min accepts and expects the degradation that everyone imposes on her, and she has no aspiration, no vision of herself, except the bare instinct to survive. By contrast, Lutie knows who she is and what she wants. She has aspirations for herself and her family, she has a strong sense of independence and high self-esteem. She is a Negro lady seriously in pursuit of worthy ideals. Placed in the context of overwhelming adversity, Lutie is made of the stuff that all heroines are made of.

But the concrete circumstances of both Lutie and Min contain the same social realities. First and foremost, both of them are black women. Secondly, although Min more so than Lutie, both are victims. They are regarded by society and by the men of both races as nothing but sex objects. Both are poor and are denied better employment opportunities because of their sex and their color. Both are "domestic servants" working for white folks who view black women as nonpersons and promiscuous whores. They live in the same building and the same neighborhood. Altogether, because of their sex and race, they are subject to the same general oppression. But when it comes to their inner worlds, to their attitudes and their character, they are completely two different women—almost.

[11]

The origins of the differences in the psychology of Lutie and Min are complex and yet quite simple. There is the age difference in the years of their experiences. Min is forty or more. She has been demeaned and stepped on all of these years. From what has been ascertained about women who come to be like her, Min is almost certain to have been sexually abused and battered during her childhood. Her household was probably one in which battering and quite possibly incest and alcoholism occurred. She may not remember some of the incidents, since they were so horrible when experienced that they are unbearable, resulting in "blank spots" in order to deny and shut them out. Then, too, Min's complexion is black, her features are blatantly Negroid, and she has been treated as being "ugly" all of her life—and has been made to feel that it was all her fault. This is especially so since she is not only black but a female too. Therefore, all of her experiences have inflicted in her a "double negative" concept of herself. Plus, she is of obvious common, peasant background, of little education, and has been so persistently tortured that she has been rendered inept and left with only the barest instinct for survival. As mentioned, Min is any number of women in the pages of fiction written by black women. She is Pecola in Toni Morrison's *The Bluest Eye.* She is the young Celie all over again. She is Eva in Gayl Jones's *Eva's Man.* Min is herself, and at the same time she represents untold numbers of black women in real life whose stories are never made public.

It is significant that Lutie, *and* Min, are both protagonists of *The Street,* as it is significant that the two women, although victims of the same oppression, are completely divorced from each other. Lutie was married when she was seventeen, and when the novel opens she is barely in her twenties. Although her Pop drank a lot and regarded women like all men regard them, and though no mention is made of her *mother* (no mention was made of Bigger's *father),* there is no evidence that Lutie experienced any abuse as a child. She has a brown complexion, which meant that she could "stick around," whereas if she had been solid black, she would have had to "get back." Through the "luck" of being not exactly the "wrong hue," Lutie enjoyed some "good fortunes" which Min was denied. She therefore was permitted to acquire a sense of self-worth. At one point of extreme frustration, she cries out, "What possible good has it done to teach people like me to write!"

But the most glaring difference in the psychology of Min and Lutie is *class.* Not class in the material sense, because both women are in the same boat when it comes to the reality of their lot—they are poor. But class in the sense of orientation and identification. Min's inner world may be described as comprising a set of what Richard Wright called "dim negatives." She possesses a victim psychology, a consciousness that sums herself up as being nothing but a "common, nigger wench." Lutie Johnson identifies herself with the "better class" of colored people. She knows racism has rendered her people the way they are. But at the same time she disassociates herself from the "niggerhood" imposed on them and inflicted in them, and she harbors a middle-class bias toward them. When she discovers Bud, her son, with a shoe-shine box, she admonishes him and expresses her wish for him not to be "just like the rest of these niggers." Angry and hurt over her husband's being with another woman, she refers to the woman as "that black bitch!"

She exemplifies not only a class bias but a color bias against darker-skin members of her race.

Lutie's class (and color) biases may be further described as being identified with capitalistic values of the white American middle class. Working for the rich Chandler Family, she experiences first-hand the decadence in white middle-class life, the racism, Christian hypocrisy, and general "soap-opera" degeneracy of their family relations, including infidelity, incest, and suicide. She is terribly aware that America is bent on denying black people the "better things" in life. Nevertheless, she staunchly believes in the "higher values" of white America, and that she can achieve these values.

Lutie is in pursuit of the American Dream. This is her *quest*. She believes in all the virtues of the Protestant Ethic: the virtue of middle-class respectability, the virtue of hard work leading to getting ahead, the virtue of moral restraint leading to clean living, the virtue of serious personal purpose, and the virtue of thinking, grooming, dressing, and behaving "respectable"—all leading to happiness. She identifies with Ben Franklin as a model. She is determined to better her situation for herself and for her young son. She wants and demands respect as a Negro *Lady*, and she is nobody's "nigger wench."

Again, while Lutie rejects the hypocrisy and degeneracy displayed in the Chandler Family, she nonetheless wants the things they possess. She is lured by the beautiful "miracle kitchen." She reads the magazines the Chandler women read, *Vogue, Harpers Bazaar, Town and Country, House Beautiful*. Down under, she judges herself as always looking up at the standards of the whites and gauges her aspirations accordingly.

The class bias and the racial self-loathing tendency, with their innumerable machinations, are not only at the roots of the alienation between Lutie and Min. But this class bias and this self-hating tendency are at the roots of the fragmentation and disunity among black women and black people in general. Though Lutie and Min, and all the women in *The Street*, suffer the same oppression because of their race and sex, they are completely divorced from one another, and suffer in separate, isolated, invisible enclosures. Through the machinations of race and class, they are manipulated, divided, and rendered helpless against their common enemies.

But most of all, throughout the novel, over and over again, Lutie's consciousness and actions are totally dominated by the supreme value of capitalistic life—*money,* or, more correctly, the lack of money. Boots was correct about one thing. The reason Lutie plays the game with him in the first place is because she needs money. The oppressors know money can lead to independence. This is why no one does anything to help Lutie find a well-salaried job. This is why Junto instructed Boots not to pay Lutie a salary for singing in the band, but to give her "presents" instead. Keep Lutie dependent, as Min and the rest of the women are kept dependent. Though the women work as hard as anybody, they are kept virtually slaves because of the low, inadequate wages paid to them, while the men, white men first and black men last, keep all the high-status, best-paying jobs as their own. Moreover, it is Lutie's lack of money and her all-consuming pursuit of it that leads to the alienation between herself and her son, Bud, and eventually leads to his delinquency and arrest, which, in turn, exacerbates Lutie's need for the all-mighty dollar. Since Lutie is away from home slaving at the Chandlers' far into the night and away in her spare time looking for better employment, Bud is left alone. He develops "fear" of the dark, he begins to feel bereft of love, and roams the streets. He dwells in the movies, fantasizing himself as a "cop or a detective." He observes his mother tired and moody all of the time, and he thinks it is because of him. She lets him know she is worried about money. It is significant that Bud's response, as a male child, is to buy his mother a "present," something he has doubtlessly learned from his sex group. Jones exploits the situation between Bud and Lutie. He tricks Bud into doing "detective work," stealing mail from the boxes in the halls of buildings along the street. The "detective work" fits Bud's movie fantasies. Then Jones "fingers" him to the cops. Though Bud is under age, Lutie is led to believe she needs $200 to free her son, for the lawyer's fee.

[12]

In racist capitalistic America, the ever-binding necessity for money is a divisive, deadly trap for black people. Yet, it is altogether foolhardy to expect black people to renounce the only way of life that they know, that they are born into and is all around them and is constantly being glorified as the American Dream. In *Dark Ghetto,* Kenneth Clark wrote:

> It would be psychologically naive and even cruel to ask the oppressed to transform the values of American culture. Before they can be motivated to try, they need to experience those values for themselves with all the satisfactions and all the frustrations and anxieties. (p. 109.)

In her unrelenting desire and quest for the American Dream and the equally unrelenting denial of that dream to her, Lutie becomes a classical tragic heroine, flawed by her virtues and fated for doom. Lutie Johnson is an Invisible Woman. No one will see and accept her for what she is and wants to be. Her travail is the saga of a Native Daughter in search of the American Dream. She is a black Womanchild in a white Promised Land.

But Lutie Johnson is not only a native of, and contradicted by, a racist capitalist world. She is also a native of, and contradicted by, a sexist world. The bind she is in is a triple bind, her oppression is geometric.

Throughout the novel, a plethora of evidence shows that Lutie is possessed by negative loyalties, just like Min and the other women. Herein lies the third tragic element in her character. In all oppressive situations, it is deemed a virtue for the oppressed to identify with the world-view of the oppressors. The oppressed are "praised" and "rewarded" for loathing themselves and for admiring their oppressors; they are derided, made to feel ashamed, and are punished for embracing any ways they themselves might develop, and are instructed and forced to manifest allegiance to the ways of those who oppress them.

The chief symptom of negative loyalty is self-blame. Though Lutie prides herself on being a lady and puts up a vigilant strug-

gle as a human being, she constantly blames herself for the bad
things that happen to her and her family. Like the rest of the
women, black and white, she firmly believes that it is wrong for
a woman to work; "it is not good for the man," she is told. She
works simply because she is forced to. Jim, her husband, de-
stroys their marriage, but Lutie blames herself. Jones set up her
son, Bud, but Lutie blames herself for being a "single parent"
away working instead of being at home. She gets angry at men,
but in the end she always finds a way to excuse them and blame
herself. She has completely identified not with any values that
might be considered women's ways, but with the values and
prejudices of the male world as pertaining to women's role and
women's nature.

Lutie is by no means blind to the rippling effects of racism on
black people, on the men in particular. Sitting in Junto's bar, she
observes and laments the effects of this racism on her people,
and vows that she will fight her way out of the hole that racial
oppression has put her people in. Furthermore, toward the latter pages of the novel, she begins to see that racism had perhaps
falsely divided the races, the women in particular, and that capitalism was the real common enemy. In the Children's Shelter
where Bud was being held along with other boys of all races,
Lutie observes that all the mothers, black and white, were as
poor as she.

But when it comes to the role that both white and black
sexism and patriarchy play in the oppression of women and
specifically in her own oppression, Lutie Johnson is blind as a
bat.

Just as black male culture socializes black men to be sexists,
black women are socialized to internalize sexist assumptions and
prejudices. Again, instead of the urge to kill her husband for
sleeping with another woman, Lutie has the urge to kill the
woman and calls the woman a "black bitch." Min does the same
thing, she blames Lutie for the increase in Jones's barbarity.
Lutie feels guilty for everything bad happening to her, especially for having to work and leave her child alone. Her granny
schooled her on the fact of being "pretty." She had better hurry
up and get married, which Lutie did. Like Min, Lutie too believes "a woman alone didn't stand a chance." But a woman

with a man is repeatedly proved not to stand a chance either, and Lutie is forced to be alone anyway, forced to work. Otherwise, she would rather be in a lady's proper place, in a nice middle-class home, servicing husband and children. Her desires, similar to the desires of most women, are simply to live the liberal life, free of the more brutal perpetrations of men. Writing in *No Crystal Stair*, Gloria Wade-Gayles made the following observation:

> . . The artists write from a feminist perspective, but their characters are like most black women in real life. They are essentially traditional in their approach to life. They do not seek new definitions of sexual roles. Most of them . . . are willing to observe the old rules. . . . Their desires for wider options . . . are essentially . . . "alternatives to brutality". . . . They want love, acceptance, respect, and, for several women, the freedom to express their creativity. Even when they realize that the "old rules" are by definition obstacles to these desires, most of the women would rather take their chances with the "old rules"; and struggle in small ways for a new reality. They live what most women live—lives of contradiction. . . . The contradiction is the result of their loyalty or conditioning (or both). . . . (p. 241.)

Lutie and the other women in *The Street* seem to be utterly mystified as to what is happening to them. But we see it plain as day. In black and white, the reader sees it all.

[13]

The Street is a frontal presentation of the sexual politics in the relations between black males and black females, the politics of male power over female existence. Ultimately, when she is on the verge of being actually raped by this power, Lutie explodes.

> . . . everything that had served to frustrate her . . . the dirty, crowded street . . . the rows of dilapidated old houses . . . the small dark rooms . . . the long steep flights of stairs . . . narrow dingy hallways . . . the little lost girls in Mrs. Hedges' apartment . . . the smashed homes where the women did drudgery because their men had deserted them. She was all of these things and struck out at them . . . Jim and the slender girl she'd found him with . . . the insult in the moist-eye glances of

white men . . . the unconcealed hostility in the eyes of white
women . . . the greasy, lecherous men at the Crosse School for
Singers . . . the gaunt Super pulling her down, down into the
basement . . . she was striking at the white world. . . .
(p. 266.)

Notice, however, that as she explodes she lays the ultimate
blame on the white world, still not fully aware of, or not daring
to declare, that black men have it within their own power to
refrain from brutalizing black women. Even when she discovers
Boots's wallet bulging with money and that he "could have
given her two hundred dollars and never missed it," Lutie still
seems incapable of condemning him as a black man. She is loyal
even as she ironically bludgeons him to death with the phallic
symbol of women's oppression, a sharp iron candlestick. Wade-
Gayles comments on this "negative loyalty."

> . . . to challenge the sexual limitations raises fundamental ques-
> tions that affect the women's personal lives, and the persons they
> challenge are often the men they love and whose children they
> have borne. . . . They often find themselves alone when they
> challenge sexual oppression. In fact, myths about women are so
> basic to our culture that women who attempt to reject them
> totally must reject a part of who they are. (p. 147.)

Clearly Lutie is "split in two" by what she is forced to do. This
is why she "explodes" in the act of killing. All the love-hate,
loyalty-resentment detonate out of her, for as Lutie kills Boots,
she is also killing a part of herself. Wade-Gayles writes:

> . . . the challenges to sexism and racism made by black women
> in the seventies were perhaps explosions of many years of sup-
> pressed resentment . . . public images are so fundamental a
> part of our reality that to repudiate them totally is tantamount to
> repudiating a part of ourselves. (pp. 147, 242.)

Finally, Wade-Gayles writes that "we cannot cure an illness by
denying that we suffer from its symptoms."

[14]

That *The Street* is a pioneer work of womanist/feminist protest is unmistakable. But it does not go beyond protest. What Alice Walker's novel *The Color Purple* does for rural blacks in the South, *The Street* achieves for black people in the urban North. However, unlike in *The Color Purple*, Ann Petry's novel does not offer any positive process of affirmation and overcoming. Lutie revolts but she revolts alone; it is an emotional, unplanned revolt—she explodes.

In 1968, twenty years after Lutie Johnson explodes, two black psychiatrists, William Grier and Price Cobbs, published a best-selling study entitled *Black Rage*. They devoted fifteen pages to black women in a chapter entitled "Acquiring Womanhood," in which they made glaring Freudian endorsements about the value of "feminine beauty and narcissism" for black women, and discussed how hard it is for black women to feel beautiful and narcissistic in white racist America.

Nothing is mentioned in the entire book about the *rage* black women might feel from the political, economic, and sexist oppression that they suffer. The only concern black men have for black women is that the women feel beautiful, be good mothers, and provide and experience good sex.

The explosion of Lutie Johnson foreshadowed the necessities for the more positive processes of black women's liberation. The modern successors of Ann Petry are busy depicting and mapping out these processes: the coming together of all women in sisterhood; the organizing and raising of consciousness; acclaiming the value of womanist ways and women-identified women; the naming of women's oppression as *sexism;* the affirmation of nurturing women, blues women, such as Shug in *The Color Purple*, Mattie in *The Women of Brewster Place*, and the women in *The Salt Eaters*, to mention but a few. This is not to take away from Petry's novel. The issues are all there, precisely and painstakingly detailed. What is needed are the solutions and the tactics. One of the women in the beauty parlor sees Lutie near the end of her rope, burdened and filled with the blues, and the woman remarks, "Somep't must have walked over your grave."

The explosion of Lutie Johnson marked her own death as a Negro Lady Heroine and initiated a new life as a Black Woman Hero. The explosion of Lutie Johnson, the murder she committed, is being transformed by today's women writers into a positive act of love and liberation. Bigger Thomas killed Mary Dalton and Bessie Mears with only thoughts of fear and trembling. Lutie Johnson killed Boots Smith in an explosion of pent-up rage against the oppression of herself, against the oppression of Min, against the oppression of all black women and all black people.

FOUR

Black Women
in the Life and Work
of Langston Hughes

FEMINISTIC WRITINGS OF A MALE POET*

Langston Hughes, born in 1902, began writing in his early youth and continued until his death in 1967, by which time he had published a vast body of literature. The poet Sarah Webster Fabio once said that Hughes "was for fifty years the spiritual leader of the Black race." Since his death, writers, students, teachers and scholars have turned out a steady stream of material dealing with the richly varied aspects of his life and work. But in the articles, essays, books, and doctorial theses, no specific attention has been given to perhaps the most important influence in Hughes's life and one of the most persistent features found in his work—the sensibilities and presence of black women.

That such an important facet in the life and literature of a renowned black writer has been categorically ignored is at best

* The present version of this chapter is a revised writing of a previously published article in *Survival and Renewal* (World Fellowship Publication, 1980), co-authored with Adriene Canon. I wish to express my indebtedness specifically to Canon and also to Jacqueline Berrien and Alice A. Passer.

unconscious. Since male chauvinism has been an integral feature of the black literary world, it is quite "natural" that no one, certainly no male, would think of the greatness of Langston Hughes's contribution to black culture in feministic terms. Even when the sensibilities of women in his work are abundantly plain, students, scholars and admirers have not seen it, because they are blinded by the biases of masculine aesthetics, masculine education, perceptions and loyalties.

It is time then to show from Hughes's own writings the various kinds of black women he wrote about, and that, far from being an aberrancy, Langston Hughes's "feminist consciousness" was an intrinsic part of his rearing and lifelong dedication to his heritage and his people.

In 1940, Hughes published *The Big Sea,* which was a straight autobiography of his youth. In this work three types of women are discernible as being dominant in his early years: (1) his grandmother, Mary Sampson Patterson; (2) his mother, Carrie Hughes; (3) the blues women celebrities he admired, Bricktop Ada Smith, Florence Emery Jones, and others.

Throughout Hughes's writings there are three recurrent images of women, each corresponding more or less with the three types who influenced his early life. I have assigned to each of them a symbolic name: (1) the "Earth Madonna," corresponding to Hughes's grandmother; (2) the "Troubled Woman," corresponding to Hughes's mother; (3) the "Blues Jazz Woman," corresponding to celebrities and "street women" Hughes knew or met.

[1]

Earth Madonna. Hughes's grandmother, Mary Sampson Patterson, attended Oberlin College in Oberlin, Ohio, where she married her first husband, Sheridan Leary, who was a freedom fighter and gave his life at Harper's Ferry during John Brown's raid. Mary was the daughter of an Indian mother and a French trader-merchant father in Fayetteville, North Carolina. Her father had been active in hiring slaves so they could purchase their freedom from their earnings and also in giving aid to fugitive slaves who had run away before the Civil War. So, long before she married her husband, Sheridan Leary, Hughes's grandmother had strong convictions about human freedom, passed on to her by her abolitionist French father and no doubt by her Indian mother as well. Hughes reports that his grandmother was a very proud woman who never begged or borrowed anything. Later in life she was honored by Teddy Roosevelt, having been invited to sit on the platform with the President as the last surviving widow of John Brown's raid.*

It was this woman who nurtured, raised, taught him and served as Langston's mentor for the first twelve formative years of his life. Mary was thoroughly dedicated to the cause of black people, and she instilled in her grandson a profound admiration for black folk. Often she would hold the young Langston on her lap and tell him long, beautiful stories about people who wanted to make the Negroes free.

In his novel *Not Without Laughter* (published in 1930), Hughes recreates his grandmother in the character of Hager Williams and recreates himself in the character of Sandy, the grandson. But there are differences between the two grandmothers. Hager Williams, the fictional grandmother, is an uneducated black woman who washes white folk's clothes for a living, a "domestic." Mary Patterson, the real one, was educated and never took in laundry and she "looked like an Indian." Hager is a churchgoer, emphatically Afro-American in appearance, speech and mannerisms. Mary, though she was a Christian, did not attend church regularly and she spoke perfect English. Nevertheless, the basic Christian beliefs, the personal dignity and the convictions about blackness are the same in both grandmothers. The only real difference is, according to Hughes, that these qualities have been exaggerated in the fictional grandmother to make her appear more typically Negro.

Grandmother Hager, then, personifies the Afro-American or the black folk Christian temperament, social background and attitude toward life. She is endowed with the intuitive knowl-

* Unless specified otherwise, all references to Hughes's life, his mother, grandmother, family and relatives, fictional and real, are based on *The Big Sea*, his autobiography (Hill, Wang, American Century Series, 1963 edition), and his novel *Not Without Laughter* (Collier Books, Macmillan, 1969 edition). The poems cited and quoted are from Langston Hughes's *Selected Poems* (Vintage Books, Random House, 1974 edition).

edge and wisdom inherent in the black folk past (rural-slave life), which can best be defined as an "earth mysticism" that reflects the tolerance and faith peculiar to black life under slavery and continued oppression.

Hager Williams—despite her poverty and the austerity of the general circumstances in which she struggles—never surrenders hope. Although conditions do not permit her to be a great leader of her people such as a Sojourner Truth, she nevertheless ensures that her grandson will be such a person by giving him all her love and a sound moral and cultural foundation. She is "gwine to make a educated man out o' him and wants him to be a leadin' de people." Again and again, the grandmother tells the grandson he is "gwine to count to something in this world." And the grandson (young Langston) knew what she meant. She meant a man like Booker T. Washington or Frederick Douglass, or like Paul Lawrence Dunbar, who did poetry writing. This selfless giving, teaching and inspiration of the grandmother is something every black person can relate to, it runs deep in the life experiences of black Americans.

The grandmother's nurturing and compassion, moreover, transcends racial barriers. It is bestowed on whites as well as blacks. In her neighborhood, whenever misfortune befalls someone, colored or white, she is there to succor and comfort. Her sentiment for whites is not the subservient devotion of a mammy, but is the practical application of Christian principles. She recognizes that white men are the oppressors whose cruelty has enslaved, frustrated and denied the hopes of black people; but she is equally aware of the disease of blind hatred. "Hatin' people, you gets uglier than they is . . . 'cause hate makes your heart ugly." According to the grandmother's philosophy, "there ain't no room in this world fo' nothing but love, Sandy chile . . . nothing but love."

The grandmother is the source of great benevolence, comforting and inspiring all who turn to her. Hence, the prototype of the image of the woman the grandmother represents is that of the Earth Madonna.

Attention should be focused on the prefix "earth," because it connotes Humanity. Unlike the conventional Judeo-Christian and Catholic Madonna, the Earth Madonna is not a cold idolized paragon, but is a fecund woman who creates and nurtures black life. Her essence is maternal rather than devotional. She births, she instructs, she inspires. Nowhere does Langston Hughes make her character more evident than in his poem "The Negro Mother." Here, the labor and sacrifices of all black women—how they were brought over from Africa, forced to work as slaves, and how they kept on fighting and struggling so their children could someday be free—are embodied in a single black woman, "The Negro Mother." In the last few lines of the poem the mother encourages her offspring to march ever forward, break down bars, look upward at the sun and stars, her dreams and prayers will impel us up the great stairs.

> Children, I come back today
> To tell you a story of the long dark way
> That I had to climb, that I had to know
> In order that the race might live and grow.
>   . . . .
> I am the child they stole from the sand
> Three hundred years ago in Africa's land.
>   . . . .
> I am the woman who worked in the field
>   . . . .
> I am the one who labored as a slave,
> Beaten and mistreated for the work that I gave—
>   . . . .
> But God put a song and a prayer in my mouth.
> God put a dream like steel in my soul.
>   . . . .
> I *had* to keep on! No stopping for me—
> I was the seed of the coming Free.
> I nourished the dream that nothing could smother
> Deep in my breast—the Negro mother.
>   . . . .
> Oh, my dark children, may my dreams and my prayers
> Impel you forever up the great stairs—
> For I will be with you till no white brother
> Dares keep down the children of the Negro Mother.

In *Not Without Laughter,* Hughes writes that the grandmother and grandson would often be alone; he might be sitting on her lap behind the hot stove in winter, the black washerwoman with the gray hair and the little brown boy . . . slavery-time stories, myths, folktales like the Rabbit and the Tar Baby; the war, Abe Lincoln, freedom, years of faith, love and struggle filled the grandmother's talk while stars sparkled in the far-off heavens. In a poem, "Aunt Sue's Stories," Hughes depicts the same situation.

> . . . .
> Summer nights on the front porch
> Aunt Sue cuddles a brown-faced child to her bosom
> And tells him stories.
>
> Black slaves
> Working in the hot sun,
> . . . .
> Singing sorrow songs on the banks of the mighty river
> In the flow of old Aunt Sue's voice,
> The dark-faced child is quiet
> Of a summer night
> Listening to Aunt Sue's stories.

The drama between black madonna and black youth occurs again in yet another famous poem by Langston, "Mother to Son."

> Well, son, I'll tell you:
> Life for me ain't been no crystal stair.
> . . . .
> But all the time
> I'se been a-climbin' on,
> And reachin' landin's,
> And turnin' corners,
> And sometimes goin' in the dark
> Where there ain't been no light.
> So boy, don't you turn back.
> Don't you set down on the steps
> 'Cause you finds it's kinder hard.
> Don't you fall now—
> . . . .

The analogy of life to a great staircase alluded to in "Aunt Sue's Stories" and in "The Negro Mother" is repeated and developed further. Once more the mother's intention is to edu-

cate and inspire. Life for her ain't been no crystal stair, but all
the time she's been a-climbing on.

The Earth Madonna's capacity to inspire makes her seem
more divine than human. She is a woman nevertheless. The
lines from "The Negro Mother" tell us that she was the seed of
the coming free, in her breast she nourishes the dream that
nothing could smother. The words "seed," "nourished" and
"breast" allude to her humanity. Indeed, throughout the poems
—"Aunt Sue's Stories," "Mother to Son," and "The Negro
Mother"—there is a strong interplay between the Earth Madonna's humanity and her divinity: between the biological birthing
and rearing of the black race and the abiding spirituality of the
grandmother as nourisher of the *dream,* the hopes and aspirations of black people.

In still another poem, "Graduation," Hughes depicts a tired
but spirited mother testifying about the hard work she has done
and about the sacrifices she has made in putting her daughter
through school, not merely for the daughter's sake alone, but so
the entire colored race can rise.

> . . . .
> Mama, portly oven,
> Brings remainders from the kitchen
> Where the people all are icebergs
> Wrapped in checks and wealthy.
>
> . . . .
> DIPLOMA in its new frame:
> Mary Lulu Jackson . . .
> Will spell the name
> Of a job in a fine office
>
> . . . .
> Mama says, *Praise Jesus!*
>
> . . . .
> The DIPLOMA bursts its frame
> To scatter star-dust in their eyes.
> Mama says, *Praise Jesus!*
> *The colored race will rise!*
>
> . . . .
> Then,
> Because she's tired,
> She sighs.

While Ellison, in *Invisible Man*, takes time out to sing praise to "the gray-haired matron in the final row," but maintains his distance as writer and narrator, Langston Hughes completely surrenders to the feelings of the Earth Madonna. It is, moreover, the voice (the first person "I") of the Madonna speaking to us in her own words, from the viewpoint of her own experiences. It is also important to point out that in "Mother to Son," the Earth Madonna is speaking to a son, a male. But in "The Negro Mother," she is supporting and encouraging all of her "children," females as well as males—she inspires them to rise, men *and* women. And in "Graduation," the young person is specifically female, a daughter, who is the recipient of the mother's support and inspiration. As shall become more evident as we continue, Hughes possessed an abiding identification with the females of the race.

While I have been discussing the Earth Madonna in reference to the grandmother, the four poems mentioned already are about mothers, and one about an aunt. The most casual reading of the poems, however, reveals that the word "mother" is imbued with all those qualities we associate with our grandmothers, because, for one thing, most mothers, when they "mellow with age," become grandmothers.

There is a dialectic in Hughes's writing involving the Earth Madonna as the mother who is *Grand*. Even if mothers do not have any grandchildren, they become grandmothers to their own children and, whether they have any children of their own or not, they become grandmothers to all black youth, and dedicate their lives through labor and sacrifice for the uplift of succeeding generations. Throughout the diaspora of black people, in America, Latin America and the islands of the seas, the grandmother goes all the way back to slavery, to the so-called extended family and inevitably back to the Greatest Grandmother of all—Africa! It is, moreover, the special quality of wisdom acquired through endurance and survival, and the long-suffering attributes of love and faith and inspiring humanity on the part of any black woman toward the future of the race that we term "Earth Madonna." The mother who is Grand then is a historical personage in the Black Experience. She, as Earth Madonna, is the personification of the African Past, and Hughes's poems constitute her legacy to the black race. His poems also exemplify public recognition of his personal understanding of the role black women have played in nurturing him and his race, and the poems exemplify Hughes's identification with the values of that nurturing.

If the prefix "earth" implies humanity, then it also implies imperfection. In other words, there is a "flaw" in the Earth Madonna's character. Ironically, the flaw is her strongest attribute, her Christian love.

In *Not Without Laughter,* this "flaw" in the character of Sandy's grandmother, Hager Williams, is made clear in her continual bouts with her younger daughter, Harriett, who is antireligious and hates white people with a vengeance, and who loves to sing blues and dance and "hang out" in the "Bottom," where the people "get down" most "sinfully." Hager is forever chastising Harriett, whom she perceives as living a life of sin and who will go to hell when she dies. Also, Hager doesn't appreciate the good-timing itinerant husband (Jimboy) of her second-eldest daughter, Annjee (Sandy's mother). To a lesser extent the same is true of Hughes's real grandmother, Mary Patterson (in *The Big Sea),* who puts the young Langston through many trying episodes prodding him to "see" the Lord, be saved and join the Baptist Church.

On the other hand, the Christianity "flaw" in the character of the Earth Madonna is merely one of scolding and chastising and not one of rejection of her children. When Harriett gets arrested for "street walking" and later runs off with a circus, Hager does not disown her, and when the daughter returns home broke and beaten, Hager takes her into her arms and rejoices, "Ma chile! Done come home again! Ma Baby chile come home!" Again, when Sandy wants a sled for Christmas, it is Hager who goes to the moneylender, and when Annjee is sick in bed, it is Hager who works twice as hard to pay the doctor bills. Hager even likes Jimboy's singing when he puts "Christian" words to his blues tunes.

So the Christianity "flaw" is more apparent than real; yet it is real. Christianity sustains the group's faith in life and in a better day to come. But its traditional doctrine of humbleness and love-thine-enemy hinders its advocates in being more than survival leaders. At best the Earth Madonna inspires the race to revolt. She cannot lead the charge. She provides her army of youths with a garrison of dreams and prayers. But these alone cannot overthrow the white regime of racial oppression. In the final analysis the legacy of the Earth Madonna lies in her ceaseless hard work, her indestructible love, and in her noble, inspiring *voice* that resounds through the centuries.

[2]

Troubled Woman. The second-strongest influence in Hughes's life was his mother, Carrie. This is interesting because he saw little of her as a child or as a young man. The brief times they were together were spent mostly on the run, Kansas City, Topeka, Colorado, Cleveland.

Hughes's father, James N. Hughes, was possessed by a relentless passion for the almighty dollar. In Mexico he grew rich. Carrie did not like Mexico, for one thing, and soon after their marriage the couple separated (she left him), then divorced. She was married a second time, to an itinerant laborer named Homer Clarke. It seemed that the search for adequate employment kept him on the wander: Carrie trailed after him for a while; then they lived apart, formally separated, then divorced. Often the mother was alone, sometimes with her young son Langston, but always she was forced to pull up stakes looking for work, since the rich father in Mexico refused to give her any money. Actually though, Langston, in his autobiography, *The Big Sea,* does not record very much about his father, stepfather, or his mother. Yet the character and life circumstances of the threesome must have had a lasting impression on him. For, in the novelized version of his youth *(Not Without Laughter)* he writes about them at length and in great depth, particularly his mother and stepfather.

In some ways Carrie was not unlike her mother, Mary Patterson. Carrie was bright, intelligent, civic-minded, she liked plays and took her son to see them. She wrote a little, gave recitations and read papers before the Interstate Literary Society. She too believed in the rights of black people, exemplified in her successful struggle to have Langston admitted to an all-white school in Cleveland, Ohio. But she lacked her mother's enduring strength and fiber. Langston's grandmother, Mary Patterson, emerges as a semigod. His mother Carrie has a vulnerable streak. She has character, to be sure, but roots are not firmly planted in her, and though she does not have as much formal American education as her mother (only a year of college), she has been more deeply affected by the character-deteriorating effects of American "feminization," which renders black women without sufficient grounding within themselves.

Carrie, Hughes's mother, is represented in *Not Without Laughter* by the character Annjee. Again the traits of the real mother are exaggerated in the character to make her more representative of a certain kind of Negro woman. Annjee works as a "domestic" for Mrs. J. J. Rice, from early morning to late evening, seven days a week. She, her mother Hager, her younger sister Harriett, and her son Sandy (young Langston), all live in a three-room house of meager quality. They are poor and sleep double, sometimes triple when on occasion Annjee's husband, Jimboy, is in town. Although both the real and fictitious mothers are given to leaving the young son in pursuit of their men, and in lieu of work on their own, it is Annjee, the fictitious mother, who shows less familial commitment.

Annjee loves her family and son; she works hard in Mrs. Rice's kitchen, brings leftovers to help feed the family and Jimboy when he is around, and when her younger sister Harriett is stranded away from home, she digs up her savings ($2) to send to her. But in the final analysis Annjee's heart and soul, her body and mind belong to but one person—her wandering, blues-singing, carefree man, Jimboy.

Though he causes her heartache by being away from her, she loves him unremittingly. She worries and pines for him, she is nervous and jittery expecting a letter, and though he seldom writes that he is coming home or even where he is, she defends him against Hager's constant criticism of "dat good-for-nothing worthless an' wanderin' Jimboy." On her sickbed Annjee defends him. "O, don't say that, Ma," she cried weakly, "Jimboy's allright, but he's just too smart to do this heavy ditch digging labor, and that's all white folks give the colored a chance at here in Stanton. . . ."

Annjee will do anything for Jimboy. She buys on the never-never a silk shirt for him, on her two-dollars-a-week salary. There is no need to forgive him of anything because in her eyes he can do no wrong. She expresses no fear of Jimboy and other women during his long, frequent absences. And when he comes home unexpectedly (though she expects him for days, weeks, months), he spends more time with Harriett, singing blues songs, dancing in the backyard and generally rousting about, but Annjee shows no jealousy. She waits until he is ready for her. The sentiments he has for her are carefree, off-the-cuff, nothing deep. But it is him and him alone for whom she lives. She takes nothing and gives everything. Finally, she goes to him in Chicago . . . he leaves her there and goes to the war . . . she would never have thought of asking Jimboy to get a job . . . yet she demands that her (by now) fourteen-year-old and promising son drop out of school to help support them.

Self-sacrificing, self-emaciating love and ultimate devotion are the prime characteristics of the "Troubled Woman"—all for her man who, in the eyes of nearly everyone else, is a "no-good-for-nothing" man. Her life is a hard one, filled with loneliness and melancholy—because her man is usually not there, or he doesn't treat her right, or he may even beat her. But she is devoted to him, she worships him, he is her god, without him (and she is without him!) she is nothing, she may not even wish to live.

Hughes wrote a specific collection of poems entitled "Lament over Love," the bulk of which reflects the mood of the Troubled Woman—"Misery," "Cora," "Young Gal's Blues," "Hard Daddy," "Midwinter Blues," "Lament over Love," and so on.

MISERY

Play the blues for me.
Play the blues for me.
No other music
'Ll ease my misery.

. . . .

Cause the man I love's done
Done me wrong.

. . . .

A good woman's cryin'
For a no-good man?

CORA

I broke my heart this mornin',
Ain't got no heart no more.

. . . .

The ones I love.
They always treat me mean.

YOUNG GAL'S BLUES

I'm gonna walk to the graveyard

. . . .

I'm goin' to the po'house

. . . .

The po' house is lonely
An' the grave is cold

. . . .

When love is gone what
Can a young gal do?

. . . .

Keep on a-lovin' me, daddy,
Cause I don't want to be blue.

LAMENT OVER LOVE

I hope my child'll
Never love a man.

. . . .

Love can hurt you
Mo'n anything else can.

. . . .

Im' goin' up in a tower
Tall as a tree is tall,
Up in a tower
Tall as a tree is tall.
Gonna think about my man—
And let my fool-self fall.

Beyond the specific collection, throughout Hughes's poems, the lamenting voices of troubled women can be plaintively heard.

TROUBLED WOMAN

She stands
In the quiet darkness,
This troubled woman
Bowed by
Weariness and pain
Like an
Autumn flower
In the frozen rain,
Like a
Wind-blown autumn flower
That never lifts its head
Again.

MID-WINTER BLUES

In the middle of the winter,
Snow all over the ground.
. . . .
My good man turned me down.
. . . .
Don't know's I'd mind his goin'
But he left me when the coal was low
. . . .
He told me that he loved me
But he must a been tellin' a lie.
. . . .
But he's the only man I'll
Love till the day I die.
. . . .
I'm gonna buy me a rose bud
An' plant it at my back door,
. . . .
So when I'm dead they won't need
No flowers from the store.

Such utter devotion! Such sacrifice! Such self-immolation! The Troubled Woman demands nothing, not even in death.

Before her man the Troubled Woman emerges as the suffering angel. Indeed, in *Not Without Laughter*, Annjee's real name is Anngelica. She is the suffering angel of unreturned love. She lives a life of grieving and bereaving, as though her "one and only" were dead, since he is always gone from her—but she will not take another, as though she herself were dead. Why? Why is she like this? Why does she flee from warm houses and break down doors to wander naked in the cold? Is it because she is in love with "Strange Hurt"?

. . . .

> Days filled with fiery sunshine
> Strange hurt she knew
> In months of snowy winter
> When cozy houses hold,
> She'd break down doors
> To wander naked
> In the cold.

Hughes does not explain; he depicts, depicts so faithfully that within the masochistic-like wailings of Troubled Women, we see clearly that they have had the living life beaten out of them not merely by "no-good-for-nothing" black men, but by the totality of a woman-hating-black-hating society, a society that beats the breath out of all women, but triply beats down the dignity and self-worth and self-love of black women. Such that the Black Troubled Woman is rendered more submissive, more passive, more "feminized" than even her white counterpart. She now really feels that a "real" man is the one who treats her like a second-class dog, and that she is not a "woman" unless she is *dependent* on such a man. This, in large part, is the ontology of black women who are root-deprived in the urbanized racist and sexist caldron of Western civilization.

It is interestingly crucial that the men of Troubled Women are portrayed as having no identity apart from the women. Seldom do the "no-good men" appear separately from the women. We learn about the men from the women, in the women's voices and according to the women's viewpoint. "Her man" is indeed a "her-man." He is a parasite, a pimp, a deserter, and often a batterer of women. "Normally," we see women depicted only in connection with the men, as men's appendages. Hughes has reversed the case, correctly. As in the lines cited above, the women, moreover, tell their experiences and feelings in the blues format. The blues are the Troubled Woman's lot, they are also her expressions of endurance, survival, and her form of artistic protest against the hardships of life and men. In "Cora," the woman expresses disdain for the male half of the race. "Next time a man comes near me/Gonna shut an' lock my door/Cause they treat me mean—/The ones I love. They always treat me mean." And in "Lover's Return":

> Oh, men treats women
> Just like a pair o' shoes—
> You kicks 'em round and
> Does 'em like you choose.

The "her-men" means that the women take care of the men and suffer their abuse—the "her-men" play on the women's love for them, getting what they want—money, sex, shelter, food, and freedom to do as they please. Notice also how the women comply with the wishes of the men and the dictates of patriarchal culture by, for one thing, conceiving of the men as "daddies," as in "my old time daddy" and "I went to my daddy," and also in the very title of the poem itself.

HARD DADDY

> I went to my daddy,
> Says Daddy I have got the blues.
> I cried on his shoulder
> But/He turned his back on me.

Hughes shows too that the men conceive of women as "hosts," and that relations between the sexes are supposed to be male-dominating, male-exploiting relations, and the women should sacrifice themselves for the men.

AS BEFITS A MAN

> I don't mind dying
> But I'd hate to die all alone!
> . . . .
> I want a dozen pretty women
> To holler, cry and moan.
> . . . .
> I want the women to holler:
> *Please don't take him away*

Ow-ooo-oo-o!
Don't take daddy away!

GONE BOY

Playboy of the dawn,
Solid gone!
Out all night
Until 12—1—2 A.M.
Next day
When he should be gone
To work—
Dog-gone!
He ain't gone.

In "50-50," the woman laments about being all alone with no one to share her bed and hold her hand. The woman asks what must she do? The man's voice comes in and says, "Share your bed, *and your money, too.*"

Hughes shows, furthermore, that the women are troubled because they are rendered dependent on men for love. The men, along with male society and culture, reinforce and exploit this dependency. Throughout Hughes's blues poems, and the ballad ones also, the "hard-daddy" attitudes and behaviors of black men are depicted, as in "Ballad of the Fortune Teller."

He mistreated her terrible,
Beat her up bad.
Then went off and left her.
Stole all she had.

Hughes's identification with women is repeatedly demonstrated in his blues and ballad poems. He recognizes, bears witness to, and decries the injustice of the women's lot in their relations with men. Hughes, of course, would write several poems of intimate identification with the horrible suffering inflicted on Billie Holiday, one of which will suffice.

SONG FOR BILLIE HOLIDAY

What can purge my heart
Of the song

And the sadness?
Do not speak of sorrow
The sorrow that I speak of
Is dusted with despair.

Hughes also wrote the same kind of definitive poems about and in the actual voices of prostitutes, delinquents and "un-wed mothers," as in the following:

RUBY BROWN

She asked herself two questions
What can a colored girl do on the money from
    a white woman's kitchen?
And ain't there any joy in this town?

(. . . good church folk do not mention her name
    anymore . . . But the white men . . .
    pay more money to her now than they
    ever did working in their kitchens.)

S-SS-SS-SH

Her great adventure ended
As great adventures should
In life being created
Anew—and good.
    Except the neighbors
    And her mother
    Did not think it good!
The baby came one morning,
Almost with the sun.
    The neighbors—
    And its grandma—
    Were outdone!
But mother and child
Thought it fun.

Notice that the women are outcasts of society, and have experienced and are experiencing the hard knocks of life. There is no doubt where Hughes's sympathies lay. Notice, too, that the men in the poems cited, and in others, are pictured as boys hardened in the righteousness of patriarchal irresponsibility toward the women who love them and suffer their shiftless, abusive ways. For this, for telling it like it is, Hughes has often been castigated for having no strong male role models in his writings. The criticism has come from nationalistic and middle-class-oriented males, particularly from revolutionary macho-inclined males. But Hughes's view of black males in his writing is shaped almost entirely out of black women's views of men, and often their secret views of men.

[3]

The Blues Jazz Woman. Three basic variations of Blues Jazz Women appear in Hughes's writings. Blues Jazz Women vary according to differences in some combination of age, experience, class orientation, degree of country-ness versus urbanity, and specific situation with men. The first variety of Blues Jazz Women is closest to and descends directly from the Earth Madonna, and is most represented by Sister Mary Bradley in the pictorial book *The Sweet Flypaper of Life.*

Sweet Flypaper was first published in 1955, reprinted in 1967, and a third brand-new reprint was issued in 1984 by the Howard University Press under the directorship of Charles Harris. It is a beautiful and wonderful book. The photographs are by Roy Decarava and the text by Hughes. It is easily the most inspiring, heartrending book of its sort on black ghetto life. Large, bold photographs consist of women, men, children, families, groups of black people in various situations of life, both solemn and playful, stern and relaxed, private and public. The setting is Harlem. The text is narrated by the book's central character, Sister Mary Bradley, in her own words and from her own perspective on life. The narrative opens with Sister Bradley's responding to a telegram from Saint Peter. Its message is, "Come home." Sister Bradley tells the messenger boy, "Take that wire right on back to Saint Peter because I am not prepared to go. I might be a little sick, but as yet I ain't no ways tired." Later, she addresses the Lord Himself, saying, "Come home! I got plenty time to come home when I get to be eighty, ninety, or a hundred and one. . . . But right now, you understand me, Lord,

I'm so tangled up in living, I ain't got time to die. I got to look after Ronnie Belle."

Sister Bradley has several grown children and a tenth baby grandchild. Originally from South Carolina, she introduces us to all of her children and many of her grandchildren, and she narrates the story of their lives at their various stages—single, married, their work, how they look, what they wear, their habits, way of life, their concerns and relations with the community, as well as her own particular relations with each and every one of them. In the process Sister Bradley tells us all about herself, and we come to know, respect and love her as we would our own grandmother. She is very much related to the Earth Madonna personage of Aunt Hager, but she is also a progression once removed from Hager, Aunt Sue, and the Negro Mother image.

Sister Bradley is in the North, in a sprawling ghetto. While she is at heart a humanist, she is no fundamentalistic Christian. She is bold, outspoken, independent. Though she is no longer young herself, she understands and respects young people. She reports that when young herself, she used to "get down" quite a bit. So she "digs" the partying and Saturday-night festivities of her children and grandchildren, who are comfortable around her and who often ask her to sing at their parties, which she does, an old blues she remembers:

> My blues ain't pretty.
> My blues don't satisfy—
> But they can roll like thunder
> In a rocky sky.

Sister Bradley remembers being in love, and might even consider marriage again to the janitor who comes to visit her while she is ailing, and who says to her, "Miss Mary, I hear tell you's down—but with no intentions of going out."

Sister Bradley replies, "You're right! I done got my feet caught in the sweet flypaper of life—and I'll be dogged if I want to get loose."

It must be stressed that Langston Hughes is nowhere in the picture. It is Sister Bradley talking, narrating, depicting, portraying and communicating herself, her world and her views to us—they are black views and they are a woman's views. You know damn well, too, that they are Hughes's views. We never see a photograph of Sister Bradley until the very end, when she says, "As for me, well, if I do say so, I'm good as new—back on my feet again and still kicking—with no intentions of signing no message from Saint Peter writing me to 'come home.' When I get through with my pots and pans . . . ever so once in a while, I put on my best clothes. Here I am."

There she is, too: a full-page photograph, solid black, wrinkled hands and all—in a black old-folk's dress; slender but hefty, wearing earrings and a plain round black hat, standing beside a wrought-iron fence in front of a brownstone, a closed-mouth smile and her black eyes shadowed by the brim of her hat—looking straight at you! You can tell, and you know from the manner in which she has presented herself and her life, that she has never been so helplessly dependent on any man's so-called "love" that she would permit that man to walk all over her. After all, God is a man, He is the Almighty Man, and she told Him she was not going anywhere yet. Part-rural, part-urban, folkish with just enough citified-ness to be "moderen," Sister Bradley represents the first generation of twentieth-century black women migrants from the South who have adapted to the ways of the North. She stands on her own two feet, still in possession of her soul, her blackness and her womanness.

The second progression of the Blues Jazz Woman in Hughes's writing is Madam Alberta K. Johnson. She has owned a beauty salon and a barbecue stand. By being a proprietor, signifying her independence and enterprising abilities, she has gone one step further than Sister Bradley and planted her feet in the men's world. Hughes wrote a dozen special poems in Madam's own voice of the black folk-urban vernacular. The first poem is entitled "Madam's Past History," in which Madam introduces herself to us.

> My name is Johnson—
> Madam Alberta K.
> The Madam stands for business.

She tells us about her businesses, how she prospered until the Depression came, and also until she got mixed up with a "no-good man." Because she had "a insurance," she was denied assistance from social security, and she retorted, "DON'T WORRY 'BOUT ME! . . . I'll get along." She concludes the introduction by repeating, "Alberta K. Johnson—*Madam* to you."

Madam employs herself out as a "day worker," and she does cooking also. Although she has lived a checkered life, Madam Alberta K. lets the world know that she will not accept any abuse. She believes in fairness, she will be fair with you and you must be fair with her. In "Madam and Her Madam," her employer tries to work her like a mule, and Madam says, "Can it be you trying to make a packhorse out of me?" When the woman replies that she loves Madam, Madam retorts,

> That maybe true—
> But I'll be dogged
> If I love you!

In "Madam and the Rent Man," the landlord's agent calls to collect overdue rent. Madam recites him all the repairs that have not been done, and ends the encounter by telling the agent, "If it's money you want you're out of luck." When he says he is not pleased, she tells him that neither is she, "So we agrees."

All of the twelve poems are in a similar vein, Madam either wins out or maintains her ground.

When it comes to men, and people in general, she demands mutual fairness and respect of person, nothing more, but nothing less either. In the past she adopted two charity children but had to give them up because of hard times and bad luck with raising them, a girl first and then a boy. The severity of life has taught her to maintain a tough exterior. In "Madam and Her Might-Have-Been," we learn that she has had two husbands and "could of had three—but my Might-Have-Been was too good for me." She has grown up the hard way and knows that "sometimes you don't know what's too good to be true just might be so." She dismissed the man because she has come to believe that "nobody loves you for yourself alone."

Madam has had so many bad experiences in life that she is

cynical and critical of most people, including herself. Boldly independent, forthrightly dignified, Madam is an aggressive black woman who stands up for what she believes is right, derived from the "hard knocks" of experience, tempered by common-sense wisdom. Similar to Sister Bradley, in "Madam and the Wrong Visitor," she tells death in a dream that she is not going with him, and awakes from the dream asking for a big plate of chicken. She demands to be called *Madam*, not "lady." She is a womanish woman. When the census man comes and tries to convince her either to make the "K" mean a word or leave it out of her name, she, claiming it makes her name too short the way it is, retorts,

> I said, I don't
> Give a damn!
> Leave me and my name
> Just like I am!
> Furthermore, rub out
> That MRS., too—
> I'll have you know
> I'm *Madam* to you!

Although the K does not stand for a word, it represents a part of Madam, a part of who she is—and all parts of her are vital.

Though Madam is alone and fends for herself, in all of her poems, including "Madam and the Minister," Madam delights in her independence and thrives without submitting to the indignities of men and society. She is not bitter or resigned to some wretched fate. Rather, she simply will not allow societal perceptions and ascriptions to alter her image of herself. A "domestic," she works hard and fairly, and does not see why her work should be degrading or dehumanizing. She performs it with dignity. It is a means to fulfill desires and necessities without negating other important aspects of her life.

Madam Alberta K. Johnson maintains a certain moral standard for her conduct without pretentiousness and without feeling it is necessary to put on "airs." She is no starry-eyed romantic. She is nobody's "lady-in-waiting." She is an existential woman. She does not "reflect" any man ("Rub out that MRS."). A man who desires her will have to meet her terms, fair terms.

She has not allowed the lack of sex or love to destroy her soul, her life, herself, and make of her a "junky" for men. Cynical of being "set-up for the kill," she turned down the last man, who swore he loved her for herself alone. Though she could well be, she is not a woman-identified woman, not yet. She will accept nothing less than equality with men, and hardly any man can stand equality with a woman. Madam is an urbanized, modernized version of Blues Jazz Women who are alone and like it. They are women who are refined and have adapted themselves to coping effectively with the realities of their lives. Though her circumstances are less than ideal, she will "get along." Madam is *Madam* to the world.

The third and ultimate progression of Blues Jazz Women in Hughes's work is the Wild Woman. The Wild Woman is really a Warrior Woman. Proud, belligerent, and beleaguered by the strictures of culture, state, racism, sexism, and all the controlling forces and institutions of society, the Warrior Woman lives a defiant life. She breaks free, to become her own woman. Unlike her earlier kindred spirits, however, the Wild Woman variety of Blues Jazz Women prefers the anonymous lights of the hazardous night to the "security" of family and homeplace.

In *Not Without Laughter,* the Warrior Woman is represented by the character Harriett, youngest daughter of Hager, sister to Annjee, and aunt of Sandy (the young Hughes). When Jimboy is around, as we have mentioned before, Harriett is more of his pal, his equal, than is his wife, Annjee. Harriett and Jimboy sing, dance, and make merry around the house and in the yard. Harriett will not have a "respectable" job: waiting on tables, cleaning silverware, washing dishes, ironing linen, scrubbing floors on her knees, or doing any of the usual work ascribed to black women—"that's too much of a good thing!" she declares. Cognizance has already been taken of Hughes's concentration on and his empathy for the masses of black women who are forced to labor in that semiservitude called "domestic employment." But, characteristically, Hughes is as faithful to the portrayal of the Harriett variety of women as he is to the rest.

Harriett's women and men friends are denizens of Pearl Street in the notorious "Bottom," where good-timers, gin drinkers, blues singers, jazz players, and women like her do their things. She is one of them. She dresses in red silk stockings, bright and shimmering to her hips, her skirt ending midway between her ankles and knees—the type of clothing her mother, Hager, describes as "shameless bad gal's dress." Harriett tells her mother, "Your old Jesus is stiff and don't like niggers to have a good time and make them afraid to even laugh on Sunday." Harriett's older sister, Tempy, is middle-class to the bone and is ashamed of under-class, "common niggers." Because of his father and the middle-class relatives in Washington, D.C., Hughes harbored a fierce hatred for middle-classness in anyone and anything. In *Not Without Laughter,* his portrayal of Tempy, in all her apings of white values and mannerisms and prejudices against blacks, is a scathing caricature in black "bourgeoisie-nerr."

Accordingly, Harriett is aware that when niggers get up in the world, they act just like white folks—don't pay you no mind . . . well, she didn't want to be respectable if she had to be stuck up and "dicty" like Tempy was. Unlike Annjee, who is light-brown, and Tempy, who is very light, Harriett is coal-black, like her mother Hager. She has paid her dues for her complexion. As a little girl in an integrated school, she was ridiculed by her white schoolmates—"Blackie, Blackie, Blackie!"—who segregated themselves from her once they left the building. "O, I hate 'em!" she cried. "I hate white folks. I hate 'em all!"

[4]

Hughes's straight autobiography, *The Big Sea,* published in 1940, is a record of his youth. He talks about the idiocy of his middle-class relatives in Washington. In his novelized version of his youth, he typified them in the character of Tempy. More importantly, the novel, *Not Without Laughter,* published in 1930, is an odyssey of a young man's journey through early life, in which each character represents a different genre of life and a different attitude toward life in the historical spectrum of Black Existence.

From Earth Madonna to Troubled Woman, the Wild Woman

is the third persona of Blues Jazz Women. The progression is not a straight line but is dialectical. Earth Madonna represents the basic black folk Christian tradition; Troubled Woman personifies the suffering blues motif; and Warrior Woman is a progressive fusion of positive attitudinal elements of both of the above and yet freed from their repressive strings, such that she emerges as the archetypical blues-jazz tradition of black women in the development of American society and culture. She is out in front of both of her sister variations, Sister Bradley and Madam Alberta K. Johnson. She lives by her wits, she survives not by making peace with mean forces but by improvising and rebelling. She is not a creature of the culture. Rather, she is a mover and a creator of culture. At the level and quality of her existence, the Wild Woman is free and alone. She is not worried about living respectably; to do so would be to assist in her own enslavement. She is a rioter in the streets, the would-be revolutionary in the wing, the radical black feminist in the making.

The Wild Woman is thoroughly familiar with at once the white culture and her own black culture; she is familiar with the blues and jazz and with the ways of the world. And she knows the machinations of the three *isms.* Her freedom is high-priced, and she knows it. Hence, unlike the Earth Madonna, the Troubled Woman, Sister Bradley and Madam, the Wild Warrior Woman can be and is often more given to black rebellion. When, for example, Annjee wants Sandy to drop out of school to help support them by getting a job, Harriett admonishes her sister: "This boy's gotta get ahead—all of us niggers are too far back in this white man's country to let any brains go to waste . . . he must be able to help the black race, Annjee! You hear me? Help the whole race!"

Again, though she is more Westernized than the other women, the Wild Woman's black cultural insides govern her inclinations; and her style, her walk, her speech, her gestures are infused with the rhythm of Africa. Hughes often likened her to an African queen. Describing Harriett, the fictitious aunt turned blues singer, he writes: "She enters the stage in a dress of glowing orange, flame-like against the ebony of her skin, barbaric, yet beautiful as a jungle princess." Writing of Florence

Emery Jones, Hughes calls her a brown-skin princess who swept across the floor like a handsome tigress.

In his straight autobiography, *The Big Sea,* Hughes says that he never had an aunt who ran away with a carnival and later became a sensational blues singer. He says, though, that he always wanted one! The Warrior Wild Blues Jazz Women in his poems and other writings are primarily drawn from the blues singers he knew and admired as well as from "women of the street" he saw everywhere he went, and with whom he experienced an immediate identification. He wrote a plethora of blues poems largely in the voices of women. In his ingenious innovative book of jazz poetry, *Ask Your Mama; Twelve Moods for Jazz,* Hughes devotes one of the twelve sections (moods) to the trials and triumphs of the great Dinah Washington. The reality of Dinah's life and songs are spelled out in plain terms; at the same time she and her music are lifted into the realm of the legendary and mythological; Dinah becomes a hero of the souls of black folk.

Hughes grew up during the 1920s, when the great women blues singers came on the scene—Bessie Smith, Mamie, Laura, Clara, Trixie, Ida Cox, Mama Yancey, Victory Spivy . . . alas, Billie Holiday. Hughes felt these women, the songs they sang and the life they lived were the bearers of the entire legacy of the Black Experience in the New World. Then, too, because of lack of space, the young Hughes often slept in the bed with his mother Carrie at various periods until he was fourteen years of age. In *Not Without Laughter,* depending on how many people were sleeping in the house at any particular time, the little boy, Sandy, sleeps often with his grandmother Hager, his mother Annjee, or with Aunt Harriett. Of Sandy, Hughes wrote:

> He was a dreamy eyed boy who had grown to his present age (14) largely under the influence of women—Annjee, Harriett (and) his grandmother (Hager). . . .

Langston took unto himself the songs and sighs of the sufferings and joys of black women. The blues for Hughes were the quintessential cry of black life. Blues singers were the messengers who gave this cry its form, its power and beauty; and it were the women who touched Langston Hughes most. They led a racy existence full of grit, glamour and glitter, and too often grit again. It was the life they lived and their philosophy of that life that characterized the Wild Warrior Women in Hughes's work. After a woman mourns the death of her lover, she suddenly realizes: *"Yet you never can tell when a woman like me is free!"* The woman in "Hard Daddy" ends her blues by singing

> I wish I had wings to
> fly like the eagle . . .
> I'd fly on my man an'
> I'd scratch out both his eyes.

And when a woman's wandering lover returns infirm and ready to die, the woman ends her lamentation with "Damn a lover come home to die!"

These are not Troubled Women singing. Rather, they are the Wild Women in the nightclubs, on the stages and in the streets, singing the blues jazz songs for their sisters who are yet repressed and burdened down. Blues Jazz Women all share a common soul. But unlike the Troubled Woman, the Blues Jazz Woman is neither emaciated by men nor by society. The Troubled Woman is either silent or she sings the blues alone to herself within the enclosure where the world never hears her and out of whose prison she seldom breaks free. On the other hand, Wild Women are vocal to the world, they are in a continual process of revolt; being "free within themselves," men and the world interpret them as being "wild" and "untamed;" or, as Shirley Chisholm would say, "Unbought and Unbossed." Like Hughes himself, Wild Women assume the liberty and responsibility of speaking out for the millions of their sisters who have neither the liberty nor the voice to live or speak freely.

Within the context of the big three isms—sexism, racism, and capitalism—the life of the Wild Woman is precarious at best. Because she voices the strife and woes of her own life as well as those of the lives of her sisters, men and the world seek to cut her down. The Wild Warrior Woman thrives on neon lights that will spotlight her and then more quickly cut her down. Hughes understood the defiance of Blues Jazz Women because he, too, was a rebel. He also realized the imminence of the "backlash." The Earth Madonna and the other Blues Jazz Women survive to the extent that they make compromises with society at some point or another. The Wild Warrior Blues Jazz woman takes her freedom, but always at the risk of being wasted.

[5]

By way of summary, the following women appear prominently throughout Hughes's writings:

> The Earth Madonna
> The Troubled Woman
> The Blues Jazz Woman
> a) Sister Bradley
> b) Madam Alberta K. Johnson
> c) The Wild Warrior Women

There are other kinds of women in Hughes's work, but he wrote about the above ones the most. He had an affinity also for gospel spiritual singers, for they were equally singers of the souls of black women, and of black people, as were the rest. He wrote the first gospel musical produced on Broadway, *Tambourines to Glory,* with the great gospel singer Sister Rosetta Thorpe starring in the lead. Someway, somehow, there will always be people trying to put Hughes down for identifying with women and for living and writing the way he did in general. The more "learned" ones will allude to something being "wrong" or "lacking" in his childhood and impute a "pathological factor" about his inclinations. Hughes was more than accustomed to this. Certain people will definitely find something "wrong" with you when you identify with and speak out for the oppressed, especially for women. A black female student in a Langston Hughes's seminar class said,

> I have been quite impressed by the vigor and depth of Hughes' female characters and I think that this aspect of his writing makes him rather unique among the other writers of the Harlem Renaissance, and among Black male authors and poets generally. Quite extraordinary, the myriad unnamed women of his blues poems is a remarkable literary achievement, and his women comprise an important, substantial, and unique element of his work.

In the mid 1950s, a tired black woman "domestic" boarded a public bus in Montgomery, Alabama. When ordered to get up and let a white man sit where she had sat down, the woman refused and was dragged to jail. A decade later, in the mid 1960s, when Black Power and Black Revolution reigned in the streets under the leadership of the strongest macho black men, Langston Hughes published his last book of poems in 1967, *The Panther and the Lash.* He dedicated the book to "Rosa Parks, the woman who started it all."

I believe that as a committed voice of oppressed people of the world, Hughes felt most like the women whose sex is by far the most oppressed, the triple-oppressed, and Hughes rightfully portrayed and decried the oppression of women as much as, if not more than, the oppression of men. The distinctly feministic awareness and sensitivity of Hughes enabled him to assume the voices of women as easily as the voices of men. As will be shown in the next chapter, poetry is the primal distillation of the music of all people. Hughes is within the tradition of the black oral narrative folk forms and genres, and he innovated and extended these forms without hesitation. Though he was born a male, a consideration of the woman-identified nature of Hughes's writings intrinsically belongs within these pages.

FIVE

Black Women Poets

THE ORAL NARRATIVE TRADITION

In chapter Two I stated that black women poets in particular constituted a formidable phalanx of the conscious-raising activities of the 1960s. The fact is—as with the singers of spirituals, gospels, blues, jazz, and rhythm and blues too—it was the women poets who, although unrecognized, sang the souls of black people through the centuries and pioneered in the 1960s the movement toward the articulation of their truer lives, resulting in today's bonanza of black women's literature. The six books listed here are a cross-sectional representation of the

Toi Derricotte. *Natural Birth.* The Crossing Press, 1983. 60 pp. $4.95 (paper).

Brenda Marie Osbey. *Ceremony for Minneconjoux.* Callaloo Poetry Series. University of Kentucky, 1983. 86 pp. $5.00 (paper).

Thulani Davis. *Playing the Changes.* Wesleyan University Press, 1985. 64 pp. No Price Given (paper).

Colleen J. McElroy. *Queen of the Ebony Isles.* Wesleyan University Press, 1984. 91 pp. No Price Given (paper).

Cheryl Clarke. *Narratives: Poems in the Tradition of Black Women.* Kitchen Table: Women of Color Press, 1983. 55 pp. $4.95 (paper).

Rita Dove. *Museum.* Carnegie-Mellon University Press, 1983. 77 pp. No Price Given (paper).

rapid-fire activity of black women poets whose works underpin and amplify the contemporary scene.

It is fitting to begin with Toi Derricotte, because her book is an in-depth rendering of the most primal of human experiences, an experience which one half of the human race cannot know: birth.

    i
grew deep
in me
like fist and i
grew deep
in me
like death
    and i
grew deep
in me
like hiding in the sea and
i was
over me
like
sun and i
was under
me
like sky and i
could look
into myself
like one
dark eye.

Listen closely to Derricotte's rhythm in her labor, listen to the beat, the cadence in the meaning of what she is experiencing:

I-aah	grew deep in me	like FIST	and
I-aah	grew deep in me	like DEATH	and
I-aah	grew deep in me	like HIDING in the sea	and
I-aah	was over me	like SUN	and
I-aah	was under me	like SKY	and
I-aah	could look	into MYSELF like ONE	

DARK EYE.*

---

* This is my restructuring of Derriocotte's structure to emphasize the vaginal auditory depths of existentially experiencing the creating of another being.

Inside of her (w)hole self—which becomes ONE DARK EYE
witnessing CREATION—Derricotte is ultra-awake to the existential transformations of her being bringing forth another being:

i was so
beautiful. i
could look
up in the
light and
see my huge-
ness,

. . . .

. . . when i
was so deep
in myself
so large
i had to
let it out

. . . .

. . . i
dropped back
on the table
panting,
the sudden visibility—
his body,
his curly wet hair,
his arms
abandoned in that air,
an arching, squiggling thing,

. . . .

a son is born.

. . . .

this lump
of flesh,
lump of steamy
viscera.

. . . .

i lay back, speechless, looking
for something
to say to myself.

Natural Birth is a first-person narrative. It begins with the
seventh month of pregnancy. Derricotte arrives at a maternity

home to be turned away for lack of space, *i.e., no room in the inn!*
A place for her is found in a home with a family. Finally, she is
admitted to the Holy Cross Hospital. There, along with other
pregnant girls, the experiences of going through labor and giving birth to her son are related in phenomenal detail. Ranging
from straight prose to prose-poetry to exquisite verse, the writing is bold, gutsy, unpretentious, and convincing; it is at once
awesome, confrontational, and humbling. At the time (seventeen years ago) Derricotte is but a girl, and like the other pregnant girls in the hospital, she is "unwed." But she is, or pre-
tends to be, tough, romantic, and idealistic, vowing to keep her
child and to be a better mother than her mother. She would

> . . . finish school at night . . . would not hurt like all those
> women who screamed and took drugs . . . would squat down
> and deliver just like the peasants in the field, shift my baby to my
> back and continue . . .

She shares her "tough" attitude with the other girls and admonishes them to "stop believing in their mother's pain." Birth
could be beautiful if they would only believe that it was beautiful and right and good. Soon, however, the pep talk gives way
and reality catches up with the idealistic [tough] would-be-peas-
ant girl Derricotte: *pain is as common as flies.*

> going to the bathroom . . . sit on the toilet . . . press real
> hard . . . *it hurts i can't help it oh it hurts so bad!* . . . feel so
> ugly pressing down here, *shame, shame!* . . . can't believe it
> hurts like this and getting worse. . . .
>
>   . . . .
>
> 10:29, the clock is stuck . . . stuck on pain . . .
> . . . never again, never have a baby, never believe that this is
> beautiful or right or good i'm rolling in the dark.
>
>   . . . .
>
> . . . no one to come and save me from this pain . . .
>
>   . . . .
>
> the clock goes no where . . .
>
>   . . . .
>
> each moment is a desert i must cross . . .

Derricotte's pain is eternal. It is specifically *her* pain. But it is also the pain of all women, of all humanity. Philosophically, and literally, she cries out:

> how can they know the mountain of pain in me? how can every woman suffer so? how can every man and woman walking on legs, the thousands you see each day, how can each have had a mother like me? how can life contain it? how can any woman know and let this happen? one pain like this should be enough to save the world forever.

Derricotte experiences her labor as morally messianic, and her pain takes on meaning that extends beyond herself to the universe. Under the excruciating eternity of suffering, Derricotte transcends her personal pain, she becomes multiconscious and sees herself in heroic terms. Her pain is a mountain inside of her, each moment a desert she must cross. Artificial "lady-like" discretion and repression are exorcised in and through the torment of her labor. In intimate fits of vernacular images, she indicts the pain-inflicting mores of the phallic world, poised over her in the form of the obstetrician.

> doctor comes in . . . a hammer up my cunt . . . wants to feel the damn thing's head . . . *this is the one who told me i would hurt.* FORGET ALL THAT SILLY BREATHING STUFF. YOU'LL TAKE A SHOT LIKE THE REST WHEN THE TIME COMES . . . sticking his whole hand up my asshole . . . like sticking a wooden ax handle up my cunt and grinding it inside me, hot cigars burning ax handles . . . raping me . . . his whole gloved hand up my wounded cunt.
> . . . .
> he must be happy to make me feel such pain . . . because he is a man . . . in control of me . . . wants me to roll and beg like a dog. . . . (p. 27.)

In the middle of this rather horrifying passage a sudden transcendental illumination pierces through:

> my heart is open. my whole body is open . . . my mouth, each mouth inside me is open and bleeding. each heart is like the moon without a middle, a white hole in the sky so wide the sun has gone through.

Natural Birth is Toi Derricotte's second book—her first collection is entitled *The Empress of the Death House* (1978)—and her works are in a number of anthologies, including the outstanding black feminist anthology *Home Girls,* edited by Barbara Smith. In this anthology she writes that her now seventeen-year-old son asked her if she'd read *The Scarlet Letter.* She replied with a poem entitled "Hester's Song." In it she wrote:

> i rode you piggyback
> through groundless sky,
> the stars white foam in my face.
> they wanted to drive you
> back to namelessness,
> were jealous of the thought of you
> for which the universe
> convulsed wide open
> and made a cave.
> 　　. . . .
> at night i curled over you
> guarding my rage,
> i thought you might escape
> through the crown of my head
> like a chimney.
>
> i lay without husband
> 　　. . . .
> you are the one gold
> ever to come of alchemy.

Like most contemporary black women's poetry, Toi Derricotte's is the poetry of liberation and testament. Unmistakably female, or, if you will, *womanist,* it continues and begins anew the oral-narrative-poetic tradition of Maria Stewart, Sojourner Truth, and Frances E. W. Harper in the nineteenth century, followed in the early twentieth century by Georgia Douglas Johnson, Effie Lee Newsome, Helen Johnson, Anne Spencer, Gwendolyn Bennett, and a host of others. The tradition belongs to the general tradition of all black writing, the origin, nature, and function *(i.e., Aesthetics)* of which derive from the social circumstances—slavery, segregation, discrimination, injustice, and brutality—in which black people have lived. But owing to the historically extraordinary oppression (sexism, racism, class-

ism) of women of African descent in the New World, the literary tradition of African-American women is a special tradition,
one that has often been suppressed and ignored. More than half
a century ago, Georgia Douglas Johnson wrote:

> The heart of a woman goes forth with the dawn,
> As a lone bird, soft winging, so restlessly on,
> Afar o'er life's turrets and vales does it roam
> In the wake of those echoes the heart calls home.
>
> The heart of a woman falls back with the night,
> And enters some alien cage in its plight,
> And tries to forget it has dreamed of the stars,
> While it breaks, breaks, breaks on the sheltering bars.
>
> (Langston Hughes & Arna Bontemps, eds.,
> *The Poetry of the Negro; 1746–1970.* p. 73.)

This tradition constitutes the legacy handed down from generation to generation of black women writers, and it is the heritage out of which contemporary black women poets are writing,
including the six under consideration. Their poetry deals with
the elements of women's lives and women's aspirations in wom-
en's terms: childbearing, girlhood, aloneness, love and unlove,
deaths, survivals, dreams, struggles, transformations.

[2]

The first book of poems by Brenda Marie Osbey, *Ceremony for
Minneconjoux,* is steeped in this tradition, as if the youthful Osbey were two or three hundred years old.

> sometimes
> i am this lone woman
> standing in a field
> where only weeds
> survive
>
> . . . .
>
> i plant words
> and bring up myself
> even if no one sees me

> i can be the history of migrations
> coming up through city pavements
>   . . . .
> surviving in settings
> where even wild parsley
> can not grow.

While Derricotte speaks in her own personal voice, out of and about her own personal pain and glory, Brenda Marie Osbey's *Ceremony for Minneconjoux* consists of the lives and experiences of many different women. They are young girls, adult, and aged women; some of them are single, others are married; variously they are sisters, daughters, mothers and grandmothers. While each of them speaks in her own voice, they are all definitive personages of the historical continuity of black women, whose collective voices are underwritten by the distinctly masterful oral-narrative-poetic style of Brenda Marie Osbey. Some of the women tell the stories of other women as well as their own. The first to introduce herself is "felicity."

> my name is felicity
> i live inside the city
> i am telling only
> as much as you can bear.

felicity (no capital "F") tells about the "bahalia women," and in the process she (Osbey) skillfully reveals her own self.

> these women mean business
> burn their hair only on the ends
> and spit tobacco
> in the reverend's hedges
> they call themselves
> mothers
> and wear bare feet in public
>
>   . . . .
> and i have seen them dancing
> along the interstate in mid-January
> we call them madhouses
>
>   . . . .
> i know their secrets
>   . . . .

> journey with me and see what i see
> . . . .
> but when you make the final journey
> and stand at the crossing
> seeking the barred footing
> it was i who first showed you
> and remember my name
> it was felicity who told you
> how to exit one madhouse
> and enter the other

All of Osbey's women are "crazy," salt-of-the-earth women whose personas and voices are flavored by the "quaint" heritage of the cultural melting pot of New Orleans. In addition to influences from the American Indian and French and Spanish cultures, the styles of speech and the general aura of the women reflect a certain African mystique ("primitive" ways and "superstitions") carried over into the New World and blended with the indigenously developed folkness of Southern black women. Imbued thusly, Osbey's "madhouse" women are destined to reveal conditions and experiences that other, "nicer," more "lady-like" women are not permitted to reveal, but which are not uncommon in the lives of just about all black women. Exhibiting the salient ingredients of all great narrative poetry, the lives of the women are not only their actual lives, but they equally assume the aura of mythological lives, wherein the voices of individual women are communally amplified and raised to epic significance. The title poem, "Ceremony for Minneconjoux," is a fine example of this, and is introduced by the voice of an omnipotent narrator:

> it was years back you know
> down bayou la fouche
> she named her daughter
> minneconjoux
> so that people would not mistake
> her indian blood

Faithful to the folk method of Tall Tale Narratives, the omnipotent (or communal) voice soon slips into the voice of an unidentified first person, "I." In a controlled yet free-wheeling, episodic, back-and-forth, commentator fashion, "Ceremony for Minneconjoux" dwells on various characters and events while talk-telling, stage by stage, the threads in the history of the life of the first person. Only at the very end does the first person formally identify herself as minneconjoux, the teller of the tale.

> i am minneconjoux
> i live in the house on st. claude st.
> i connect myself
> to the used thing
> i keep on my bureau
> at mardi gras time
> i stand on the walk-way
> and watch the indians
> dancing off dumaine.

The method of moving from community (omnipotent) narrator to individual (personal) narrator, and vice versa, is characteristic throughout *Minniconjoux,* and is particularly noticeable in "The Factory Poem":

> somehow when i talk of feelings   [CALL]
> some gut
> seems to jump into what i say
> all up in my mouth
>
>   . . . .
>
> what did she know of freedom,
> chained to some memory
>
>   . . . .
>
> a dead man moving around
> inside her body
> and her whispering to him
>
>   . . . .
>
> *woman*   [RESPONSE]
> *i said i heard you*
> *heard you had trouble in the mind*
>
>   . . . .
>
> i have been drained of myself   [CALL]
> on warm winter days
> i resort to a violence
> that teaches you the meaning
> of words like
> hurt.

> . . . .
> *i said i heard you*　　　　　　　　　　　　[RESPONSE]
> *heard you had trouble in mind*
> *yes i heard you*
> *woman*
> *i done heard you[r] mind.*

The italicized lines are analogous to what the European tradition refers to as "chorus." In the African tradition those lines are the *response*. The unitalicized lines constitute the *call*. Of course, the italicized lines are *blues,* and "Trouble in Mind" is a traditional blues. Unlike the tradition of the spirituals and gospels, which are religious and are collective expressions of the black community that touch individual lives, the blues is a secular solo vehicle speaking to the collective experiences of the community through expressions of the single individual. In the folk-oral-narrative poetic tradition of Afro-America, *Ceremony for Minneconjoux* is a mosaic, a *quilt,* of many varied individual yet collective lives of New Orleans black women.

LIVING IN THE TAN HOUSE

> . . . .
> and what did i know—
> a girl of nineteen
> knowing what a grown man of thirty-seven should do?
> we married then
> and two years later
> he bought this unsightly house
> and had it painted tan
> people coming into the neighborhood looking at me
> the old folk would say
> "lavinia, miss thierfield's daughter?
> "she's living in that tan house up the street" . . .
> was how everybody called it
> "that tan house"
> and so did i
> . . . .
> but i needed something
> i really did just need something
> . . . .

and that was how i discovered my throat and
commenced to singing
people'd say
"lavinia, ms. thierfield's daughter,
we never knew she could sing before"
they never did
because i never did
till one night my throat opened up
and i commenced to singing
it was like hearing a language that never had been
it was like having a whole other woman
standing in your middle
singing out your insides.

WRITING THE WORDS

the sky gives witness to history

    . . . .

i can see sally
stitching her bald head
to the back of her womb

    . . . .

and when i can no longer testify
i will stitch open my eyes
i will stitch them to my fingers
and together
they will witness the history
and hand down the tale

For a first book, Brenda Marie Osbey's *Ceremony for Minneconjoux* demonstrates extraordinary artistry and command of down-home-folk techniques and modalities. Osbey's heritage, of course, is the eclectic richness of French-, Spanish-, African-American folk culture of New Orleans, the stomping ground of the legendary conjour woman, "Leveau."

[3]

The tradition of narrative-chronicling the exigencies of black life in America began during slavery and took the form of spirituals, or, as W. E. B. Dubois called them, the Sorrow Songs. *"Nobody Knows the Trouble I've Seen." "Sometimes I Feel Like a*

Motherless Child. " The first literary manifestation of the tradition was expressed in the autobiographical narratives of nineteenth-century fugitive slaves who fled northbound on the Underground Railway and in the early novels and abolitionist oratory of escaped slaves and free Northern blacks alike. Following Reconstruction, with the rise of the KKK and other hate groups, an inordinate amount of violence was let loose in the South against black folk. Not only were their lives maimed and suppressed but their very ethos was maimed and suppressed. In order to survive the onslaught of uninhibited racism, the entire cultural tradition of black folk, both musical and literary, went underground and for several decades wore various disguises. Due to "jim crow," wholesale lynchings, and the plague of "boweevil" in the South, and pulled by an unprecedented demand for labor in a North getting ready for war on a world scale, once again the first two decades of the twentieth century witnessed millions of blacks fleeing the South to the North in search of a-better-day-a-coming. Like an ever-unwinding umbilical cord, the tradition migrated up the Mississippi and dispersed into St. Louis, Kansas City, Memphis, Cleveland, Chicago, Philadelphia, New York. By the 1920s the tradition had reconstituted itself in the form of blues, ragtime, and jazz, and Scott Joplin, Ethel Waters, Ma Rainey, Bessie Smith, Langston Hughes, and Zora Neale Hurston were its new champions. In his classic novel *Mumbo Jumbo,* Ishmael Reed refers to the resurgent outburst of black culture during the 1920s (formally labeled the New Negro/Harlem Renaissance) as "Jes Grew." The seed of Jes Grew remained the same, but its style and complexity were transformed by and to accommodate the new environment of the Northern cities.

This, then, is the tradition out of which contemporary black women poets are writing, and it constitutes the heritage and legacy that inform the bulk of their work, in which the profoundly simple narrative of black country folk is extended and further developed in order to express the conditions of contemporary life in the Northern environment. *Natural Birth* expresses the meaning of giving birth in terms of one woman's experience, and is waterbreaking, if not in style, definitely in its candidness. *Ceremony for Minneconjoux* speaks the lives of many

women in the mode most closely associated with the black coun-
try-folk narrative, distinctly flavored, though, by the New Orleans cultural milieu and the individual freshness of the poet's
astute skill.

The poetry of Thulani Davis and Colleen J. McElroy, on the
other hand, represents the more advanced narrative poetic di-
versification of the tradition. Their poetry is in the upbeat mode
of the complicated riffs, breaks, and contrapuntal cacophonies of
city life, city struggle, city politics, city corruption, city dreams,
and city agonies, and, most of all, the driving craze for dollar
bills, warm as bedspreads, cold as icebergs.

The titles of both Davis's and McElroy's collections bespeak
the new situation. *Playing the Changes* and *Queen of the Ebony Isles*
amplify the old tradition in the new language and cadences of
jam sessions and jazzy rhythms of panoramic forces that impinge
on and characterize black life in urban settings. "Ebony Isles"
are ghettos—and "Playing the Changes" is "hip-talk" for ma-
nipulative improvisational behavior along the alleyways, stoops,
and concrete streets where abrupt changes and deathly hazards
are commonplace.

Davis's first poem sets the new motif, from the country communal scenes of the South to urban cities full of alienation, iron
and concrete, factories and nightclubs and fancy new ways; from
earthy folks to "contessas & cardsharks."

> slick boys and cardsharks,
> baffled local prophets,
> cane-colored contessas
> with orange-black hair
> crowd over a kitchen table.
> professional elegants
> out of work
> they could hum you some Monk
> or tell you about when Malcolm
> was a child

These are urban boys and girls, citified men and women. The
poem traces them from their 1920s Southern rural backgrounds
through various social and political movements, from Garvey-
ism to Malcolm X. The poem goes on to exemplify worldly

awareness, the situation in Africa and the role of the Pope; it signifies the role that black music—Leadbelly, Monk, reggae—has played in connection with the adoption of new styles of black life, *romantic chroniclers/gambling/dabbling in dope/experts in gruesome details.* The poem ends with a statement on the effects of black people always forced to be on the move in an endless diaspora: *it's hard to stay in one piece . . . ask those scrawling on walls.*

The key poem to the diaspora-motif in *Playing the Changes* is "north of the last place, west of the first," a long, jazzlike narrative on the triangular slave trade, a "Middle Passage" type of poem, in which the refrain echoes like the sound of ocean waves: *we are going perhaps/but nowhere/we know about.*

> our destination became a deep river
> on the other side of the tracks
> a gal named Sal, Treemonisha or Aretha
> a fellow named My Guy
> our place jumped at Woodside
> raised up out of churches
> and ways of folks
> named Malcolm and Fannie
> each one a village, each one
> all time gone
> each one a tongue, a drum,
> a whole land
> a reason to live
>
> . . . .
>
> in the new place
> old as we have become
> we are going

Ever since black people were taken out of Africa they have had to be on the move, in flight from injustice, in search of wholeness, of community, of home. But it has been hard to stay in one piece. Instead, the pieces themselves, the fragments of hope have been their destination. "Deep river" refers to the spiritual by the same title, and "other side of the tracks" refers to blacks' always being forced to live in some ghettoized section of town. Yet each individual, each incident in their lives, each item of culture has constituted a village, a memorial happening, a voice that bespoke wholeness and inspired survival of the race: *old as we have become/we are going.*

Thulani Davis is a New York City woman who works for *The Village Voice.* In order to relate to her references, one ought to be "hip" or worldy-wise, because much of the poetry in *Playing the Changes* is littered with references to black personages, and there is an abundance of citified ("city-wise") imagery and metaphor. In the lines quoted above, "Aretha" refers of course to the soul singer Aretha Franklin, "Fannie" is Fannie Lou Hamer, and "My Guy" refers to the famous black rhythm-and-blues song by the same title. Minus the explicit political ideology or rhetoric, in many of the poems the subject and its treatment suggest feminist undercurrents. One example is "in the fire lane."

> the men with unhealed wounds
> jump us, try to maim us
> without even taking the bread
> without even, as Wesley says,
> anything "motivational"
>
>   . . . .
>
> did we hear the scream in the hall
> or Ntozake say, "every three minutes"
> did i know the woman
> who met the mugger
> on the same night
> was shot for saying no
> like i did
>
> he took my head
> in his hands
> and bashed it to the wall
> "yes, that's right, bitch"
> smacked off my glasses
> his brass ring cut its way
> through my mouth to the gum
> moved my teeth
> "i'm gonna kill you"
>
> i thought i was a doll
> with a porcelain face
> shattering off
>
>   . . . .

Again, one has to be city-wise to handle the references. "Bread" means money. "Wesley" probably refers to Wesley Brown, novelist and author of *Tragic Magic*. "Ntozake" is Ntozake Shange, poet, novelist, and author of the controversial feminist choreo-poem *For Colored Girls*. And "every three minutes" refers to the national frequency of muggings and/or rapes.

Like the poetry of Derricotte and Osbey, a great number of poems in *Playing the Changes* are devoted to young females. The poems of Davis, however, deal with the capriciousness of street life in big-city environment; they depict experiences of growing girls written from a perspective that highlights the exploitative attitudes and abusive behavior of boys and men toward the female sex. The line "i thought i was a doll with a porcelain face shattering off" depicts the physical battering of females by males and makes graphic imagery of the attendant psychological fragmentation—"porcelain face shattering off"—in the personality of women. And, in the poem, "boppin' is safer than grindin'," Davis depicts the philosophy adopted by young girls to protect themselves in the "war of the sexes" characteristic of urban environments.

> i danced on "Shop Around"
> but never the flip side
> "Who's Lovin' You"
> boppin' was safer than grindin'

The hit recording "Who's Lovin' You" signifies a proprietary monogamous relation in a close-up, belly-to-belly "grindin'" dance that symbolizes or leads to sexual intercourse, and is shunned in preference for "Shop Around" dancing where the girl and boy are free and aloof, symbolizing relations in which the "boppin'" dance does not obligate the girls to have sex with or become the exclusive property of any male. Intermittently the poem is punctuated with warning against the various hazards of boy-girl interaction, including the likelihood of getting battered.

> beware of slow dances and pretty men
> . . . .

> & oh wow when his kneecaps cracked
> on the ceramic tile
> as my head hit the dishwasher
>   . . . .
> . . . i flew
> off the bed/landed on my head
> on the far wall nearly dead
>   . . . .
> beware of slow dances, pretty men,
> kitchen tile and fallin' out of bed

The poem ends with the declaration of a "pact."

> not to bruise each other
> or kiss each other with all we've got
> cause boppin' is safer than grindin'
> & i'd rather dance to "Shop Around"
> than "Who's Lovin' You"

While *Minneconjoux* and *Natural Birth* are faithful to the inner world of black women's experiences and flavored with female affirmation, there is more explicit feminist, direct confrontation, anti-sexist treatment in the Davis book than in either Osbey's or Derricotte's work. Highlighting the various issues of male inhumanity to female, *Playing the Changes* is predominantly a black *womanist* collection of poems. In "Bad Brains, a band," Davis begins with:

> the only person i ever met from southeast DC
> was genius who stabbed her boyfriend
> for sneaking up on her in the kitchen
> she was tone deaf and had no ear for French

Davis poetically analyzes and depicts the psycho-sexual makeup of women-hating males in two poems entitled "misogyny (1)" and "misogyny (2)." The latter of the poems specifically portrays the sexual fascism of young black men.

> They dressed like women and preferred to
> kiss men. They allowed themselves to
> remember embraces, not as they were but as
> they wished they were. They knew no
> women. Grown women were the reason, after
> all, that a good man needed a good man. . . .

> The young boys with tender hearts. . . . One
> dressed as the virgin mary, one as a
> street-corner whore, and they tormented
> each other, trying the pledges of gothic
> novels against the penance of the church.
> They loved sin and dirt and low-down
> ladies and murdered themselves with
> the knives, chairs, fists and broken glass of
> young boys' cock fights.

The writing of Davis is heady feminist stuff. But it strikes me at times as being too heady, and often carelessly rushing to make the feminist point in a fashion that is a bit too "hip." Picture your face, for example, as being made of porcelain, and being shattered to bits! The shattered porcelain face might be a metaphor applicable to the composition of many of Davis's poems, reflective of the fragmented references, names, places, and occurrences that are dropped like confetti blowing in the wind, and a lot of which are personal, in-group references that are inaccessible to the reader who is not "hip." Davis's style, moreover, may be indicative of the impersonal, alienating, dog-eat-dog forces operating on and thus in the makeup of people living in big-city environments. Although I agree with the sentiments proffered in her poems, people who "play changes" are usually wheelers and dealers and are often clever, ingenious people. They also tend to be rootless and without any single set of profound moral commitments. Instead, they are caught up in the trendiness, alienation, and contradictions characteristic of city life and the psychology of its denizens. They exploit whatever trends are popular and profitable at the moment. In such an environment and between such people, there is a dearth of intimacy and a fundamental lack of good faith, as Davis indicates in "so long sugar suite."

> i will not say i love you
> it might turn into art or an excuse
> something that sounds like something
> to make it seem like something

Or as in "it's all in who you know, my dear."

> all this narcissism & silken decay
> . . . .

> they amused themselves with their torments
> even sold them in the market
> then tortured each other with flattery
> after flattery was all that was left
> when personal statements were replaced
> with good looks & fine wine
> they hired armies to decipher their dreams

And in "some choices are just compulsion," (dedicated to John Woo), Thulani Davis writes:

> get on the roller coaster
> and burn it out
> just to burn it out
> scream burn it out
>
> . . . .
>
> at my work
> i burn it out.

So much for choices, for commitments that are no more than compulsions. Also, "Playing the Changes," as a phrase, alludes to taking chances in a game of cards. I myself have been a gambler with dice and cards (does it take one to know one?). As typified in the next-to-last poem in the collection, "playing solitaire," to weather the game one must possess a spirit chillingly similar to that of a rogue.

> when i play solitaire i cheat
> i am an ace
> i shuffle the cards
> it's not that i have to
> win i just don't want to give up
>
> . . . .
>
> vicious cycles break my heart

To affirm changes is well and good. Still, one longs to witness the affirmation of that which is morally uplifting in the human enterprise. Like Davis, I do not want to give up, but, on the other hand, I do not want to cheat either. Through all the bad things, all the changes, I long to see a moral philosophy affirmative of a humanity that is native to the aesthetic guts of the tough poet, such as in her final poem, "black spaces," dedicated to the great, now dead poet, Robert Hayden.

in the black and few spaces
i find my fire
to make my own

. . . .

there prophets are common folk
who live among neighbors
and eat friendly bread
in the black and few spaces
where i can listen to you

. . . .

i can hear myself singing
songs only some of us know
truth only some of us believe
laughs not everyone can laugh

. . . .

the blackness of it makes me grin
so i could die for you
in the black and few spaces

In this poem, instead of the fragmented, jerky, cynical decla-
mations of urban noise and alienation, we hear and feel the
warmth of common folk, of friendly bread, of song and truth
and laughter, all qualities that are, even in death, ultimately
inspirational to the reaffirmation of life. While only a few poems
in *Playing the Changes* are imbued with these qualities, virtually
all of the poems in Colleen J. McElroy's *Queen of the Ebony Isles*
are rich in the pathos not only of the changes that human beings
must go through but rich in the affirmation of human life as
well. Consider the following lines in McElroy's "While Poets
Are Watching (for Quincy Troupe)."

we are poets watching
tight-hipped black girls
swing their batons
to the high-step
rhythms of vaseline-smoothed legs
while the oompahs of school bands
count march time for drill teams

. . . .

. . . we watch
until the old men have
placed their calloused feet

> on the nearest footstool
> and the girls have gum-chewed
> their mothers into silence
> these faces are familiar
> as Van Der Zee's photos
> as my mother's snapshots
> of cookouts in Uncle Brother's
> backyard or your own scrapbook
> of our high-school homecoming

The language and its rhythm are smooth and soothing, complimenting the distilled sense of continuity over successive generations of black people that are portrayed in the poem and throughout the McElroy collection. The poets are "watchers," they keep vigil and give testimony to changes in and regeneration of people that are as familiar as the poets themselves, for the poets recognize themselves a generation removed in the people to whom they now serve as witness-bearers.

Of the poets considered here, McElroy is the most seasoned in terms of years as well as in the practice of her art. Having published over half a dozen books of verse, her maturity is reflected throughout the forty-odd poems comprising *Queen of the Ebony Isles.* In "Monologue for Saint Louis," for example, the ethos of black folk in the cycle of eternal recurrence of youth and age, departure and return is humanly conveyed and affirmed.

> home again and the heart barely there when
> choked by clusters of words
> thick as the clumps of blue-black
> grapes we snitched every summer
> from the neighbor's arbor
>
> . . . .
>
> now earthworms have trellised the arbor
> and the crumbling heap of rotting black
> sticks cannot shield us from wind or words
> we are the women we whispered about each summer
>
> . . . .
>
> I am home again.

Here, too, is the sense of generation and regeneration, of dying and rebirth, of coming and going and coming again, beautifully symbolized in "clusters of words," "earthworms," "crumbling heap," and "blue-black grapes"—ultimately consummated in the line: *we are the women we whispered about each summer.* There is a special kind of homage to black heritage and continuity in these poems, a reverence, if you will, to change and constancy, which imbues McElroy's poetry with distilled wisdom of human life. In "Why Tu Fu Does Not Speak of the Nubian," McElroy declares:

> I want to fill the space
> with fat black babies
> with the veined hands of wretched old men
> and big mamas in flowered dresses
> shying away from welfare lines

This is no mere abstract romanticizing of black people. The distillation of McElroy's wisdom cries out for primal human form: "fat black babies . . . veined hands . . . wretched old men . . . big mamas in flowered dresses." The sense of homage, moreover, is pregnant with social consciousness: "shying away from welfare lines." The impressive quality of McElroy's poetics inheres in the ease and flow of her language (even the hyphenations: "tight-hipped black girls," "vaseline-smoothed legs," "blue-black grapes"); and the melodic rhythms and cadences seem as natural as the steady roll of water over a rolling countryside. Rather than an exhibition of learned poetic gymnastics, it is as though McElroy's poems have always existed as natural phenomena, such that the references, images, and metaphors are integral to the fabric and structure of the poems, and are organic aspects of the landscape depicted. Thus, McElroy's poems are rich in mergings, in integrativeness, in the roundness and wholeness of the experiencing of life. Poem after poem, I am thrilled, and my own experiencing of life is enriched by the *call of the familiar* in McElroy's work.

A sort of family reunion poem, "In My Mother's Room," is an excellent example of the call of the familiar, which I did not realize was familiar to me until reading the poem.

> . . . when i was
> a child . . .
> and my mother sprawled naked on the bed

. . . .
        I am slumped in the overstuffed chair
        watching the TV . . .
        My daughter frowns

. . . .
        fully clothed, I am as vulnerable
        as my mother . . .

        . . . .
        we are shadows of black into black

It is the depth of intimacy, the mergings of the human, that is
achieved in the poems and whence derive the familiarity of the
scenes painted, the feelings shared, and the meanings conveyed.
In the same family reunion poem, "In My Mother's Room,"
McElroy delves deeper into the theme of eternal recurrence of
black women's lives.

        one day, I will walk into this house
        lift her [mother's] flowered robe from my shoulder
        then stumble and sink onto the bed
        in perfect mimicry
        my legs will flow into the age-old patterns
        my pubic hairs will curl tightly
        into the early evening heat
        and I will breathe the labors
        of a hundred midwestern summers

            . . . .
        and I smile at my daughter's frown

            . . . .
        knowing all too soon
        she will finally
        finger her breasts
        and disappear into crowds
        of us naked women.

Queen of the Ebony Isles is a book of woman-identified poems,
deeply moving, vaginal poems full of compassion and warmth,
depicting and confirming cycles of fullness, decay, and regeneration: *big mamas in flowered dresses . . . breathe the labors of a hundred midwestern summers . . . daughters turning into mothers who in
turn bring forth daughters who become mothers . . . shadows of black
into black . . . we are now the women when young girls we whispered*

about . . . disappearing into crowds of naked women . . . into crowds of ourselves . . .

The feminism, or womanism, in McElroy's poems is so much a part of the way life is portrayed that it is natural to the texture and meaning of the poems, rather than being superimposed on them. Even the explicitly feminist ideological poems are of this same quality. In "The Dragon Lady Meets Her Match," McElroy raises a familiar feminist question: "What are the choices/a network of lace and spatulas/to keep you bedded and knee-deep in diapers." Then she states her preference, the kind of women who have been and are her role models, and the ultimate lesson she has learned.

> I prefer to fill my hands with maps
> and weapons fit for ladies of royalty
>
> . . . .
>
> but my real fate comes with the likes
> of Sierra Rose, Sojourner and Cattle Kate
> those women who never learned
> to corset their actions
>
> . . . .
>
> I have studied the acts of warrior ladies
> twice they've brought me back to life
> pulling the murderous tip
> of some lover's secret weapon from my breast

There is no mistaking the narrator for anything other than a radical feminist in league with the likes of Sierra Rose, Sojourner Truth, and Cattle Kate, warrior ladies, bold, independent, liberated, freedom-fighting women, to whom the speaker owes her life for pulling, ironically, a lover's secret weapon, a murderous tip (a tongue, phallus head, knife, or an ice pick) from the speaker's breast.

[4]

Of the six poets, the works of Cheryl Clarke and Rita Dove stick out the most from the other poets. In Clarke's case, it is because she is the only explicitly black lesbian-feminist poet of the group. There are about fifteen poems in her *Narratives: Po-*

ems in the Tradition of Black Women. All of them are of a sexual,
biographical, experiential nature. Some are no doubt autobiographical, and some are about other women. They are utterly
oral narratives, liberating and testimonial, from a lesbian-feminist perspective. "The johnny cake" strikes a major chord in the
collection.

> Death frees people for new experiences.
>
>   . . . .
>
> we arrived at the bungalow
>
>   . . . .
>
> By noon the kitchen was stacked with food.
> The rooms filled with the talk of bold
> independent women comforting the aunt
> and commending her on how well the body looked.
>
>   . . . .
>
> they were solicitous of me.
>
>   . . . .
>
> Death frees people for new experiences.
>
>   . . . .
>
> By dusk of the next day
> I had lit ninety candles
>
>   . . . .
>
> In the yard the bold
> independent women gathered
> suited in pastel and warm colors.
>
>   . . . .
>
> In the kitchen
> the aunt slides her hand between my thighs.
> The same hand she makes her dough with.
>
>   . . . .
>
> I welcome her hand inside my drawers.
> And come for the first time
> for the rest of the day.
>
>   . . . .
>
> Butter oozes from the hot and ready bread.
>
>   . . . .
>
> Death frees people for new experiences.
> I learned this at my friend's mother's funeral.

All of the narratives in the collection are bold, unembel-
lished, plainly worded, and cogent in their import. As in the

above poems, the symbolisms and references are woman-identified, sexually confronting, and anti-sexist. The idea of "bold independent women" is thematic throughout the narratives. The refrain line—"Death frees people for new experiences"— is perhaps a central metaphor of the intent of the collection, which is to expose and condemn sexual repression while providing truth, honesty, and sustenance for the liberation of black women. *Butter oozes from the hot and ready bread* constitutes a literal symbol of womanly fruition, of sexual lucidity, and political rising, for to declare one's boldness and independence in a patriarchal society is fundamentally political. Variously, the narratives have to do with the hell black women go through because of their "nappy" hair:

> "why couldn't you have *good* hair?"
> by the time mother finished pressing my virgin wool
> to patent leather,
> I was asking why I had to have hair at all.

Male brutality against women:

> claude snatched my pocketbook
> fished out the check
> saw my net was ten dollars more than his
> and beat me with my pocketbook from living-
> room floor to the bathroom tile.

Father incest-rape:

> My father gave me cigarettes
> from his commissary chest of drawers
> for the violence of his sex
> and my mother allowed me to smoke them
> for colluding her silence.

Woman-identified sexual relations and love affairs, orgasm awakening, gynocide, and virtually all of the issues raised by not just lesbian-feminist women but mostly all black women of contemporary as well as antecedent times are in these narratives.

Clarke is new at publishing poetry, and while the narratives are not particularly embellished in technique or artistry, they are solid, straightforward poems in the plain oral-narrative tradition of black women. With their publication they indicate great promise for Clarke as a poet.

What makes Rita Dove's *Museum* stand out from the other books is that the poems, for the most part, are not within the aesthetic frame of reference referred to as the black tradition. The poems in the book certainly do not follow any narrative line of the Black Experience, neither personally nor collectively. At least two-thirds of the forty-odd poems are not about black people and are not even remotely related to black culture. Consider, for example, "Early Morning on the Tel Aviv–Haifa Freeway."

> The shore is cabbage green and reeks.
> Reclaimed swamp sprouts citrus
> and tamarisk, manna to the ancients
> we were starved for miracles.
> Now a paper mill and Alliance Tires
> spill their secrets further out to sea.
>
> Along the roadside, two Arab boys
> drag a gull by the wings
> and beyond a horse belly-up in the field.
> A glider dips over us, silent, and
> gleams as it turns. We should stop
> but drive on.

Similarly, many of the poems are about foreign subjects, containing foreign references, names, and metaphors alluding to non-black, or non-Afro-American cultural heritage, noticeably European. "Catherine of Siena" is one example.

> You walked the length of Italy
> to find someone to talk to.
> You stuck the boulder at the roadside
> since fate has a door everywhere.
> Under the star-washed dome
> of heaven, warm and dark
> as the woolens stacked on cedar
> shelves back home in your
> father's shop, you prayed
> until tears streaked the sky.

No one stumbled across your path.
No one unpried your fist as you slept.

Some poems are about flora, minerals, and on abstract themes, such as, for example, "Pithos."

Climb
into a jar
and live
for a while.

Chill earth.
No stars
in this stone
sky.

You have ceased
to ache.

Your spine is a flower.

I believe and have written in several places that poets can write in any style, or out of any aesthetics, or simply write any way on any subject they damn well please. As a professor of writing, I have encountered just about every possible genre of poetic writing. All I have demanded is the most effective communication in poetic form. By this standard Rita Dove is an excellent poet with the ability to handle a wide range of subjects and to create crisp, concise lines and images:

we were starved for miracles.
Now a paper mill and Alliance Times
spill their secrets further out to sea.

. . . .

you have ceased
to ache.

Your spine is a flower.

. . . .

. . . you prayed
until tears streaked the sky.

On the back cover of *Museum*, the biographical blurb states that Rita Dove spent several years in Europe. Many of the poems are not only about European landscape but they reflect

what I hazard to call a "European sensibility." The bulk of these
poems may have what is termed "universal" appeal—that is,
they are decidedly absent of anything suggesting they were
written by a person of African, or African-American, artistic or
cultural heritage. Some of the titles of these poems are indicative of their subject matter: "The Ants of Argos," "Boccaccio:
The Plague Years," "Catherine of Alexandria," "Fiametta
Breaks Her Peace." I must emphasize again that these poems
are superb pieces of work, as another example, "Receiving the
Stigmata," will illustrate.

> There is a way to enter a field
> empty-handed, your shoulder
> behind you and air tightening.
>
>   . . . .
> The kite comes by itself,
> a spirit on a fluttering string.
>
> Back when people died for the
> smallest reasons, there was
> always a field to walk into.
> Simple men fell to their knees
> below the radiant crucifix
> and held out their palms
> in relief. Go into the field
> and it will reward. Grace
> is a string growing straight
> from the hand. Is
> the hatchet's shadow on the
> rippling green.

By the final image—"Grace is a string growing straight from
the hand. Is the hatchet's shadow on the rippling green"—the
metaphoric image of the kite on a fluttering string is ironically
and perfectly consummated.

Turning to the poems in *Museum* that deal with black subject
matter, the consciousness and the aesthetical or cultural heritage
that inform them shift from "European" to African-American.
Many of the themes treated in these poems are the same as
those treated in the other collections. However restrained,
there is a leitmotif of social protest in most of them. The exper-

tise and poetic style exemplified in them are the same as in the other "non-black" poems. The poem that opens the book, for example, the front piece, entitled, "Dusting," is about a domestic named Beulah who daydreams about her romantic unfulfillment of the past as she does her dusting chores.

> Every day a wilderness—no
> shade in sight. Beulah
> patient among the knicknacks,
>
> . . . .
>
> Under her hand scrolls
> and crests gleam
> darker still. What
> was his name, that
> silly boy at the fair with
> the rifle booth? And his kiss and
> the clear bowl with one bright
> fish, rippling
> wound!

Remorsefully, the poem ends:

> That was years before
> Father gave her up
> with her name, years before
> her name grew to mean
> Promist, then
> Desert-in-Peace.

More explicitly the protest note is sounded in a poem about the little-known nineteenth-century black astronomer and civil engineer Benjamin Banneker, who laid out the plans for the nation's capital, and who, being a black man, was labeled a fake by Thomas Jefferson after having received a letter and an almanac from Banneker. Entitled "Banneker," the poem reads in part:

> But who would want him! Neither
> Ethiopian nor English, neither
> lucky nor crazy, a capacious bird
> humming as he penned in his mind
> another enflamed letter
> to President Jefferson—

I assure thee, my dear Sir!
Lowering his eyes to fields
sweet with the rot of spring, he could see
a government's doomed city
rising from the morass and spreading
in a spiral of lights. . . .

In nearly all of Dove's poems a deep reflective mood abides.
Banneker "hums." Earlier in the poem he is portrayed as lying
under a pear tree in meditation on the heavenly bodies. Of
course he is an astronomer. But in "Dusting," Beulah is also
portrayed in the reflective mood, haunted by melancholy. Indeed, most of the poems in this collection are cast in the past,
allowing for a nostalgic aura tinted with aloneness. Even in her
more upbeat poems, Dove seems to cast within them an aura of
poetic melancholy, as in the blues singer poem, ironically entitled "Shakespeare Say."

Champion Jack in love
and in debt,
in a tan walking suit
with a flag on the pocket
with a red eye
for women, with a diamond-studded
ear, with sand
in a mouthful of mush—
poor me
poor me

I keep on drifting
like a ship out
on the sea

. . . .

every song he sings
is written by Shakespeare
and his mother-in-law.
I love you, baby,
but it don't mean
a goddamn thing.
In trouble
with every woman he's

ever known, all of them
ugly—skinny legs, lie gap
waiting behind the lips
to suck him in,

. . . .

my home's in Louisiana,
my voice is wrong,
I'm broke and can't hold
my piss;
my mother told me
there'd be days like this

Although the images are upbeat and jazzy ("tan walking suit
. . . a red eye for women, with a diamond-studded ear," et
cetera), Champion is alone, broke, alienated, in a foreign land;
he is dogged by the italicized blues lines that mock and render
him a sadly figure. Other poems, about family reunions, fathers
and grandfathers (Dove's own?) are also suggestive of protest
or disapproval on the part of the poet, as, for example, in "Sunday Night at Grandfather's."

He hated Billy the parakeet, mean as half-baked sin.
He hated church-going women and the radio turned
Up loud. His favorite son, called Billy
Too, had flown the coop although
each year he visited, each
Time from a different
City, gold
tooth and
Drunk.

Of course, there are lighter moments, as in "Flirtation,"
where Dove writes: "Outside the sun/has rolled up her rugs/
and night strewn salt/across the sky. My heart/is humming a
tune/I haven't heard in years!"

I like poems that make my flesh crawl, make me cry, send
chills over me, poems that affect my body, my senses, nerves,
breathing, make me sweat, stimulate my imagination, make me
think, or get angry, or break out laughing. Although many of
Dove's poems do some of these things to me, two poems in her
collection that do most of these things to me are "At the Ger-
man Writers Conference in Munich" and "Parsley." They are

long, involved narratives, filtered through Dove's black female mind's eye. The latter one deals with Rafael Trujillo's butchery of 20,000 blacks in the Dominican Republic on October 2, 1957, because the blacks could not correctly pronounce the *r* in the Spanish for parsley, *perejil.* Here is the concluding stanza.

> *mi madle, mi amol en muelta.*
> God knows his mother was no stupid woman; she
> could roll an R like a queen. Even
> a parrot can roll an R! In the bare room
> the bright feathers arch in a parody
> of greenery, as the last pale crumbs
> disappear under the blackened tongue.
>
> . . . .
>
> The general remembers the tiny green sprigs
> men of his village wore in their capes
> to honor the birth of a son. He will
> order many, this time, to be killed
> for a single, beautiful word.

By and large I find Dove an exciting black woman poet, and although she does not write out of "blackness" all of the time, she is an excellent craftswoman and is nearly always arresting. One thing is certain, she brings a different style and often a different cultural heritage to her work. Yet she is very similar to the other poets when it comes to perspective in her poems on black subjects. She is a black woman and she is not afraid to be different or versatile.

[5]

In her book *Black Women Novelists: The Development of a Tradition, 1892–1976,* Barbara Christian writes that there is

> . . . a rich and powerful tradition of black women writers . . . involving the variety and richness of the black woman's experience . . . challenging the very definition of women and . . . project(ing) their own definitions themselves . . . transforming the content of their own communities' views on the nature of woman and therefore on the nature of life . . . renewing the traditions of their communities while sustaining them . . . (they) tell the stories of their mothers . . . women who came

before them . . . the literary counterparts of their communities' oral traditions, which in the Americas have become more
and more the domain of women . . . these storytellers, both
oral and literary, transform gossip, happenings, into composites
of factual events, images, fantasies, and fables . . . critical not
only of an individual but of the entire social fabric.

Collectively, I refer to all of this as the Oral-Poetic-Narrative
Tradition of black women.

Because people talk and sing before they write, poetry is the
protoplasm of all literature and culture, it is the blood of all life.
The folk always produce, preserve and transmit an entire culture based on speech and song. The oral culture of the folk is
the foundation from which all writing springs. Poetry is the
primal human form, the instinctive response to human existence. The aesthetics and the concerns of the written literature
are contained in the oral, nonliterate foundations of a people.
Alice Walker is a poet. Almost every black writer you name is a
poet. We may never see or hear it, but they began writing poetry and will end writing poetry.

The literature of black people began on the cruel ships that
transported the Africans to the so-called New World. It began
really long ago in Africa. It simply underwent changes in the
Americas. Black poetry originated in the fields with the slave
songs. It went into the churches with the spirituals, and migrated with the blacks wherever they were scattered. When
blacks gained enough liberty to be able to write without being
killed for doing so, they took up the very forms and concerns
that had been developed in oral fashion long before writing.
The most pressing concern then as now was and is the illumination and elevation of their condition as an oppressed people.
Whether you or I like it or not, this is the principle that *de facto*
governs the aesthetic of black writing.

Black women have had to fight two battles, one against the
white oppressor and another battle against the black oppressor.
Of course, there was Sojourner Truth, along with the other
women orators and prose writers; but Frances E. W. Harper was
the foremost writing poet of the nineteenth century to sound
out the men, as in her poem "The Double Standard." As they

sang against the racist oppression, all of the Renaissance women of the 1920s continued the tradition of sounding on black men about the oppression within the race. Alice Nelson Dunbar's "I Sit and Sew," Anne Spencer's "Letter to My Sister," and Georgia Douglas Johnson's "The Heart of a Woman" are just a few examples. Then came Margaret Danner and Margaret Walker, culminating in Gwendolyn Brooks's "In the Mecca" in the 1960s, which is a poem ending with the murder of a little black girl, "Petita," by a "demented" black man. Margaret Walker had already charted the oppressive herstory of black women, and black people, in her prize-winning poem, "For My People." Then, in the 1960s, the avalanche of black women poets occurred—Sonia Sanchez, Nikki Giovanni, Carolyn Rogers, Sarah Webster Fabio, June Jordan, Audre Lorde, Mari Evan, and many more. They sounded the songs of Warrior Women! As I have noted, the most quintessential of these poets is Jayne Cortez, and a full-length study of her works is required even to begin to perceive the immensity of her contribution.

Now, while many of the above are still growing and producing—such as Sanchez, *Homegirls & Handgrenades,* and Cortez, *Coagulations*—a brand-new generation of women poets are on the scene, all of whom are within and extending the tradition. There are Stephanie Byrd and Donna Darlea, and Michelle Cliff, who has published *Claiming an Identity They Taught Me to Despise,* which is rich with the Afra-Jamaican rhythms of Negritude. I have mentioned the work of Thylias Moss, *Hosiery Seams on a Bowlegged Woman,* and the anthology by Erlene Stetson, *Black Sister.* Suffice it to mention the songs of Sweet Honey in the Rock, and the uncollected works of Donna Kate Rushin, an example of which is

> I am not a Black Goddess
> I cannot save you
> I am not a Black Devil
> I cannot destroy you
>   . . . .
> I am not a Black Goddess
> I am not a Rock
> I am not a Photograph

I am not a picture in your mind
I am myself struggling toward myself

. . . .

I am not a Black Goddess
I am not a Black Goddess
I am not a Black Goddess
I am a Black Woman
I am a Black Woman
I am a Black Woman
Do you know what I mean?

The six books, with some two hundred poems and more than four hundred pages, contain all of the richness, variety, all of the themes and issues that make up the heritage of black women's entire folk literary poetic and prose tradition. The tradition is distinctly a female tradition within the black tradition that has always sought to liberate that tradition from its misogynistic, homophobic fetters. It is a womanist tradition of the spirituals and gospels and blues and jazz and rhythm-and-blues. A tradition of Sisterhood, of mothers and daughters, of interiors and intimacies of sensual and sexual awakenings and explorations, of hurts, lonelinesses, ugliness and beauty—and of being ashamed of one's nappy edges and thick lips in a land where Caucasion standards make havoc with the features of African people. It is a tradition of events, mysteries, rites and ceremonies—a tradition of discoveries, deaths, and continuations. It is a tradition that reaches out to other lands, cultures, other women and men who are struggling against fetters and shackles, a tradition that has a truly universal empathic reach! It is a black humanist tradition grounded in affirmation rather than disaffection.

The six poets considered here, five of whom are very young, confirm that black women's poetry is alive and doing mighty well.

Epilogue

Reading the writings of black women over the years is one of the most challenging and rewarding experiences of my life. It will continue to be this way, because the literature of black women is an adventure into the unexplored regions of the black experience and the human heart.

First, there is the adventure of discovering the literature and of how it has fared through the years. Next, there is the exploring of its content and artistry. Thirdly, there is the experiencing of black women's writings as being the odyssey of the real lives of nearly all black women, including the lives of the writers.

The bibliography at the end of this book merely aims to hint at the richness of women-authored literature and how inexhaustible it is. At the least, it is shamefully unsettling to discover the enormous extent of my ignorance of this literature. By the same token, however, it has been immensely enriching to have my eyes opened to the realities of women's lives and women's feelings and the realities of all of our feelings and lives, in ways we are thoroughly trained to deny and ignore.

As an illustration of what I mean, the work of Ann Petry will suffice for one last time. Before the publication of Petry's novel, feminism had been largely "embryonic," it had been a disguised and hidden "tendency" in the bulk of women-authored literature. For all of Petry's revelations into the lives and minds of the three main protagonists—Lutie Johnson, Min, and Mrs. Hedges—Petry's greatest contribution is the haunting portrayal of the existence and the souls of the masses of NAMELESS black women along 116th Street. At a terrible price, some of them, the younger ones, seek respite in the dives along the street; most of them, the older, Christian ones, sustain their spirits through the blues, the spirituals and gospels, and in their long-suffering redemptive "Jesus." We witness these women in cheap clothes, wearily coming and going with their bundles of "hand-me-downs" and "left-overs" from white folk's closets and kitch-

ens. Some of the women have been deserted, some are battered, but for all the only source of economic survival is to be
conscripted into the ranks of "domestics." They labor in American dream homes that they will never have, and in crowded
galleys of the garment trade, in "janitorial services" and other
industrial sweatshops. The economic and political disen-
franchisement of these women is reflected in the poverty of
their lives and in the poverty of their consciousness and humanity.

All through *The Street,* Petry reminds us that these women are
our sisters, mothers, grandmothers, wives and daughters. The
ubiquitous presence of these women haunts us with the creepy
feeling that they could constitute the most formidable force of
black revolution in America—if only they were organized in
Sisterhood and asserted the collective might of their togetherness.

But the highlight of the adventure of reading Petry comes
with Lutie killing Boots Smith for being the immediate agent of
her oppression. It is chilling to witness a black woman inexorably pushed into taking the step of no return and thereby setting
herself terribly free in the world. By virtue of this unprecedented act, the black female in fiction was raised from the traditional status of a "feminine heroine" to the stature of a full-
fledged hero. She must now abandon her middle-class dreams,
her family, her son and all whom she previously knew. She will
be labeled a "murderess" and she will belong to the hunted.
But her future is wide open! Anything can happen to her, the
worst and the best. She can be caught or not be caught. She can
become a tramp, a wretched creature dying alone, or she can go
to the top of the "Most Wanted" list for becoming a revolutionary black woman in the service of oppressed people wherever
they may be.

Altogether, unraveling and pinpointing the crucial issues and
problems of urban black female experiences in modern literature and in real life, and capturing the essence of both past and
future women-authored literature, *The Street* is the primal water
of black womanist literature—it emerges as the flowing link in
the herstorical development of black women's writings and
black women's lives. What is more, Petry's writing—her prose,

her lyricism, her images, the way she works the seasons and, most of all, the sympathetic treatment of all the characters in *The Street*—Petry's *writing* stands as a literary and social achievement of umbilical significance.

[2]

Another consequence of the serious pursuit of black women's literature is the discovery of connections that I would not have otherwise made. Although they suffer a common condition and have every reason to come together, the women in *The Street* are alienated from one another. Each woman can succumb, or she can fight back. Either way, though, the women being alone and estranged from one another up north in the urban streets, Petry depicts and defines the situation in its worst terms, eventuating in its worst fate. Boots projects onto a black woman all of the hurt done to him and all of his self-hatred, too, and he persists in taking out this hurt and self-hatred on Lutie. So she, a black woman, commits the ultimate act: she kills a black man.

On the other hand, the statement that Alice Walker makes in *The Color Purple* represents the second-generation progression of the statement made by Petry some forty years earlier. *The Color Purple* takes the urban situation of *The Street* back down south among the rural folk and develops it beyond the limitations of its predicament as presented by Petry. Truly, Walker depicts the situation in harsh terms, but she also truly liberates it from the inevitability of internecine disaster—moving it from dilemma to solution. Lord knows the razor trembles in Celie's hand as she shaves "Mister." Yet she and the women overcome their condition, and not a single man is killed or injured!

The subtlety with which Walker shows how this is achieved is remarkable. Instead of "hiding" in their separate cells, the women come together in Sisterhood and overcome by nurturing each other, befriending, enlightening, sharing and loving each other, which makes each individual woman whole. This is a positive way out for both the women and the men, highlighted by Celie and Albert becoming friends in the end. She teaches and Albert listens. I am referring to the novel, not the film. Albert stops hating himself so much, and he and Celie share their thinking and feelings as only equals can do. They were never lovers. But now, at the beginning of a new day, they can be lovers—if they ever wish to.

Black writing is an evolutionary process. As a womanist writer, Walker stands in the deep waters of progression, all the way from Wheatley to Harper to Hurston, and from Petry to Dorothy West to Margaret Walker to Paule Marshall and Gwendolyn Brooks, right on up to today's writers—right on up to Alice Walker herself. While Petry's novel sounded the call and delineated the shattered pieces, *The Color Purple* responds to the call with a vision and transforms the pieces into a quilt of love.

[3]

An adventure is often filled with sadness, remorse and anger. Without warning, however, the spirit can be raised to the peaks of exhilaration. There are green things in the dark; but in the light, sparks of orange, red, purple, pink, gold and black burst and streak across the sky.

Borrowing a phrase from Eugene Redmond, the writings of black women are the Drumvoices of the legacy of our past and of the challenge to our daily lives. The women are celebrating a Fourth of July never before celebrated. In the process they are moving black literature to new frontiers, aimed, as June Jordan has put it, at "transforming the experiences of all the people of the earth."

I hope this book will contribute to this celebration and help in the transformation.

Jamaica Plain,
Boston, Massachusetts,
Winter 1987.

Selected Bibliography

Angelou, Maya. *And Still I Rise.* New York: Random House, 1978.
———. *I Know Why the Caged Bird Sings.* New York: Bantam, 1971.
Aptheker, Bettina. *Women's Legacy: Essays on Race, Sex, and Class in American History.* Amherst, Mass.: University of Massachusetts Press, 1982.
Bambara, Toni Cade, ed. *The Black Woman; An Anthology.* New York: New American Library, 1970.
———. *The Salt Eaters.* New York: Random House, 1980.
Barker, Lucins, "Color Poison." *Call and Post.* Cleveland, Ohio: March 27, 1986.
Barry, Kathleen. *Female Sexual Slavery.* New York: New York University Press, 1984.
Bauschard, Louise and Mary Kimbrough. *Voices Set Free: Battered Women Speak from Prison.* Women's Self Help Center, St. Louis, Missouri, 1986.
Beale, Frances. "Double Jeopardy: To Be Black and Female." Bambara. *The Black Woman; An Anthology,* pp. 90–100.
———. "Slave of a Slave No More." *The Black Scholar* 6 (March 1975): pp. 2–10.
Black American Literature Forum. Vol. 18, No. 4 (Winter 1984).
Black Scholar, The. "The Black Sexism Debate." Nos. 8–9, (May/June, 1979).
———. "Black Literature 85." Vol. 16, No. 4 (July/August 1985).
Bond, Jean Carey, ed. *Freedomways:* "Lorraine Hansberry: Art of Thunder, Vision of Light." New York: Freedomways 19. No. 4, 1979.
Bontemps, Arna, ed. *Great Slave Narratives.* Boston: Beacon Press, 1969.
Bradley, David. "Novelist Alice Walker Telling the Black Woman's Story." The New York *Times* Magazine. (Jan. 8, 1984).
Britton, Mariah. *With Fire.* New York: Meta Press, 1982.
Brooks, Gwendolyn. *In the Mecca,* 1968.
Brown, Tony. "The Color of Purple is White." *Call and Post.* Cleveland, Ohio: (January 9, 1986).
———. "Brown's Defense." *Call and Post.* (March 27, 1986).
Brown, William Wells. *The Narrative of William Wells Brown, A Fugitive*

Slave. 1848 reprint edition. Reading, Mass.: Addison-Wesley Publishing Co., 1969.

Butler, Octavia E. *Mind of My Mind.* New York: Avon, 1977.

Byrd, Stephanie. *A Distant Footstep on the Plain.* The Author, Boston, 1981.

Carlen, Patricia. *Women's Imprisonment: A Study in Social Control.* London, Boston: Routledge & Kegan Paul, 1983.

Chase-Riboud, Barbara. *Sally Hemings.* New York: Avon, 1980.

Chisholm, Shirley. "Sexism and Racism: One Battle to Fight." *Personnel and Guidance Journal,* No. 5 (October 1972), pp. 122–216.

Christian, Barbara. *Black Women Novelists: The Development of a Tradition, 1892–1976.* Westport, Conn.: Greenwood, 1980.

————. *Black Feminist Criticism: Perspective on Black Women Writers.* New York: Pergamon Press, 1985.

Clark, Kenneth B. *Dark Ghetto.* New York: Harper & Row, 1965.

Clarke, Cheryl. *Living as a Lesbian.* Ithaca, New York: Firebrand Books, 1986.

Cliff, Michelle. *Claiming an Identity They Taught Me to Despise.* Watertown, Mass.: Persephone Press, 1980.

————. *The Land of Look Behind.* Ithaca, New York: Firebrand Books, 1986.

Clifton, Lucille. *Two-Headed Woman.* Amherst, Mass.: University of Massachusetts Press, 1980.

Cortez, Jayne. *Firespitter.* New York: Bola Press, 1982.

————. *Coagulations: New and Selected Poems.* New York: Thunder's Mouth Press, 1984.

Coward, Rosalind. *Patriarchal Precedents.* London, Boston: Routledge & Kegan Paul, 1983.

CONDITIONS: FIVE: *The Black Woman's Issue.* Edited by Lorraine Bethel and Barbara Smith. Brooklyn, New York: Conditions, 1979.

Cruse, Harold. *The Crisis of the Negro Intellectual.* New York: William Morrow, 1967.

Davis, Angela. *Women, Race and Class.* New York: Random House, 1982.

Davis, Charles and Henry Louis Gates, eds. *The Slave's Narrative.* New York: Oxford University Press, 1985.

Deutrich, Mable E. and Virginia C. Purdy, eds. *Clio Was a Woman: Studies in the History of American Women.* Washington, D.C.: Howard University Press, 1980.

Dill, Bonnie. "The Dialectics of Black Womanhood." *Signs,* 4 (Spring 1979), pp. 543–55.

Dubois, W. E. B., ed. "Symposium; The Negro: How Shall He Be Portrayed?" *Crisis.* Vol. 31, No. 4 (February 1926), p. 165.

————. *The Gift of Black Folk.* Boston: The Stratford Co., 1924. Chapter VI, "The Freedom of Womanhood," pp. 250–73. Chapter VII, "The Negro Art and Literature," pp. 287–319.

Evans, Mari. *Black Women Writers.* New York: Doubleday, 1984.

Fahamisha, Shariet. "Black Women Writers of the USA. Who Are They? What Do They Write?" *But Some of Us Are Brave: Black Women's Studies.* Gloria T. Hull, Patricia Bell Scott and Barbara Smith, eds. Old Westbury, New York: The Feminist Press, 1982, pp. 368–75.

Gayle, Addison. *The Black Aesthetic.* Garden City, N.Y.: Doubleday, 1971.

————. *The Way of the New World: The Black Novel in America.* Garden City, N.Y.: Doubleday, 1973.

Giddings, Paula. *When and Where I Enter: The Impact of Black Women on Race and Sex in America.* New York: William Morrow, 1984.

Grier, William H. and Price M. Cobbs. *Black Rage.* London, England: Jonathan Cape, 1969.

Guy, Rosa. *The Friends.* New York: Bantam, 1983.

————. *Ruby.* New York: Bantam, 1983.

Halprin, Sara. "The Color Purple: Community of Women." *Jump Cut.* No. 31, 1986.

Harley, Sharon and Rosalyn Terborg-Penn, eds. The *Afro-American Woman: Struggles and Images.* Port Washington, N.Y.: Kennikat Press, 1978.

Harris, Trudier. "On The Color Purple, Stereotypes, and Silence." *Black American Literature Forum,* Vol. 18, No. 4 (Winter 1984).

Henson, Reverend Josiah. *An Autobiography of the Reverend* Josiah Henson. 1881 edition reprint. Reading, Mass.: Addison-Wesley Publishing Co., 1969.

Hernton, Calvin C. *Sex and Racism In America.* 1965 Doubleday reprint. New York: Grove Press, 1966.

————. "On Being a Male Anti-Sexist." *The American Voice.* No. 5 (Winter 1986).

Hooks, Bell. *Ain't I a Woman.* Boston: South End Press, 1981.

————. *Feminist Theory: From Margin to Center.* Boston: South End Press, 1984.

Hughes, Langston and Milton Meltzer. *Black Magic: A Pictorial History of Black Entertainers in America.* Englewood Cliffs, New Jersey: Prentice-Hall, 1967.

Hughes, Langston and Roy Decarava. *The Sweet Flypaper of Life.* Washington, D.C.: Howard University Press, 1984.

Hughes, Langston. *Selected Poems.* New York: Vintage Books, Random House, 1974.

———. *The Big Sea.* New York: Thunder's Mouth Press, 1986.

———. *Not Without Laughter.* New York: New American Library, 1985.

———. "The Negro Artist and the Racial Mountain." *Nation* (June 23, 1926). See also *Amistad I.* New York: Vintage Books, 1970.

Hull, Gloria T., Patricia Bell Scott and Barbara Smith. *But Some of Us Are Brave: Black Women's Studies.* Old Westbury, New York: The Feminist Press, 1982.

———, ed. *The Diaries of Alice Dunbar-Nelson.* New York: Burt Franklin, 1982.

Jacobs, Harriet Brent. *Incidents in the Life of a Slave Girl.* Reissued. New York: Harvest/HBJBook, Harcourt Brace Jovanovich, 1973.

Jones, Adrienne Lash. "Abolition and Feminism: Black Women in the Antebellum North." *New Historical Perspectives: Essays on the Black Experience in Antebellum America.* Gene Lewis, ed. Cincinnati, Ohio: Friends of Harriet Beecher Stowe House and Citizen's Committee on Youth, 1984.

Jones, Gayl. *Corregidora.* New York: Random House, 1975.

———. *Eva's Man.* New York: Random House, 1976.

Jordan, June. *His Own Where.* New York: Dell, 1971.

———. *Civil Wars.* Boston: Beacon Press, 1981.

———. *On Call: Political Essays.* Boston: South End Press, 1985.

———. *Things I Do in the Dark: Selected Poems.* New York: Random House, 1977.

———. *Passion.* Boston: Beacon Press, 1980.

———. *New Days: Poems of Exile and Return.* New York: Ebersoa Hall, 1984.

Joseph, Gloria and Jill Lesis. *Common Differences: Conflicts in Black and White Feminist Perspectives.* New York: Anchor Doubleday Press, 1981.

Ladner, Joyce. *Tomorrow's Tomorrow: The Black Woman.* New York: Doubleday, 1971.

Larsen, Nella. *Quicksand* and *Passing.* Edited by Deborah E. McDowell. New Brunswick, N.J.: Rutgers University Press, 1986.

Lerner, Gerda, ed. *Black Women in White America.* New York: Vintage Books, Random House, 1973.

Loewenberg, James Bert and Ruth Bogin, eds. *Black Women in Nineteenth-Century American Life.* Philadelphia, Penn.: Pennsylvania State

University Press, 1976. Articles by Nancy Prince, Frances Ellen Watkins Harper, Ellen Craft, Anna Julia Cooper, Frances Jackson Coppin, Charlotte Forten Grimke, Maria Stewart, and others.

Lorde, Audre. *The Black Unicorn.* New York: Norton, 1978.

———. "Scratching the Surface: Some Notes on Barriers to Women and Loving," *The Black Scholar* 9. No. 7 (April 1978), pp. 31–35.

———. *Zami: A New Spelling of My Name.* Watertown, Mass.: Persephone Press, 1982.

———. *Chosen Poems Old and New.* New York: Norton, 1982.

———. *Sister Outsider: Essays and Speeches.* Trumansburg, New York: The Crossing Press, 1984.

Marshall, Paule. *Brown Girl, Brownstones.* New York: Random House, 1959.

McCluskey, Audrey T., ed. *Women of Color: Perspectives on Feminism and Identity.* Bloomington, Indiana: Women's Studies Program, 1985.

McFarland, JoAnne. *Equinox.* Brook, New York: Hourglass Press, 1984.

Meriwether, Louise. *Daddy Was a Number Runner.* New York: Pyramid, 1970.

Meltzer, Milton. *In Their Own Words: A History of the American Negro, 1619–1865,* Vol. 1. New York: Thomas Y. Crowell, 1984.

Miller, Jeanne-Marie. "Black Women Playwrights from Grimke to Shange: Selected Synopses of Their Works." *But Some of Us Are Brave,* pp. 280–296.

Moody, Ann. *Coming of Age in Mississippi.* New York: Dial, 1968.

Morago, Cherrie and Gloria Anzaldua, ed. *This Bridge Called My Back.* Watertown, Mass.: Persephone Press, 1981.

Morgan, Robin, ed. *Sisterhood Is Powerful: An Anthology of Writings from the Women's Liberation Movement.* New York: Vintage, 1970.

Mullen, Harryette. "Daughters in Search of Mothers, Or, A Girl Child in a Family of Men." *Catalyst.* Premiere Issue. Atlanta, Georgia: Fulton Public Library, 1986, pp. 45–49.

Naylor, Gloria. *The Women of Brewster Place.* New York: Houghton-Mifflin, 1982.

Noble, Jeanne. *Beautiful, Also, Are the Souls of My Black Sisters: A History of the Black Woman in America.* Englewood Cliffs, New Jersey: Prentice-Hall, 1978.

Petry, Ann. *The Street.* Boston: Houghton Mifflin, 1946.

Redmond, Eugene. *Drumvoices.* New York: Doubleday, 1976.

Robinson, William H. *Phillis Wheatley and Her Writings.* New York: Garland Publishing, Inc., 1984.

Royster, Beatrice. "The Ironic Vision of Four Black Women Novelists." Ph.D. Dissertation, Emory University, 1975.

Rushin, Kate. "The Black Goddess." *Home Girls: A Black Feminist Anthology.* Barbara Smith, ed. New York: Kitchen Table Press, 1983, pp. 328–330.

Salaam, Kalamu ya. "Lorraine Hansberry: Unhonored as a Prophet." The *Guardian* Book Supplement (Summer 1984), pp. 8, 9. See also *The Black Collegian* (March/April, 1984), pp. 45–46; 48.

Sanchez, Sonia. *Homegirls and Handgrenades.* New York: Thunder's Mouth Press, 1984.

Scott, Patricia Bell, ed., *Sage. A Scholarly Journal on Black Women.* "Women as Writers." Atlanta, Georgia: The Sage Women's Educational Press, Vol. 2, No. 1 (Spring, 1985).

Shange, Ntozake. *For Colored Girls Who Have Considered Suicide When the Rainbow Is Enuf.* New York: Bantam, 1977.

———. *Sassafrass, Cypress & Indigo.* New York: St. Martin's Press, 1982.

———. *A Daughter's Geography.* New York: St. Martin's Press, 1983.

Shipp, E. R. "Blacks in Heated Debate Over 'The Color Purple.'" New York *Times* (January 26, 1986).

Shockley, Ann Alen. "The Black Lesbian in American Literature: An Overview." CONDITIONS: FIVE, pp. 133–144.

———. *Loving Her.* New York: Avon, 1980.

———. *Say Jesus and Come to Me.* New York: Avon, 1982.

Beck, Howard (Iceberg Slim). *Pimp: The Story of My Life.* Los Angeles, California: Holloway House, 1969.

Smith, Barbara. *Home Girls: A Black Feminist Anthology.* New York: Kitchen Table: Women of Color Press, 1983.

———. "Notes for Yet Another Paper on Black Feminism, or Will the Real Enemy Please Stand Up." CONDITIONS: FIVE, pp. 123–132.

———. "Toward a Black Feminist Criticism." *But Some of Us Are Brave,* pp. 157–175.

Staples, Robert. *The Black Woman In America.* Chicago: Nelson-Hall, 1973.

Sterling, Dorothy. *Black Foremothers.* Old Westbury, New York: The Feminist Press, 1981.

———. *We Are Your Sisters: Black Women in the Nineteenth Century.* New York: Norton, 1984.

Stetson, Erlene, ed. *Black Sister: Poetry by Black American Women, 1746–1980.* Bloomington, Indiana: Indiana University Press, 1981.

Stowe, Harriet Beecher. *Uncle Tom's Cabin.*

Tate, Claudie, ed. *Black Women Writers at Work*. New York: Continuum, 1983.

Taylor, Mildred D. *Let the Circle Be Unbroken*. New York: Dial Press, 1981.

Terrell, Mary Church. *A Colored Woman in a White World*. Washington, D.C.: Ransdell, Inc., 1940.

The Combahee River Collective. "A Black Feminist Statement." *But Some of Us Are Brave*, pp. 13–22.

Thurman, Wallace. *The Blacker the Berry*. New York: Arno Press, 1981.

TransAfrica Forum. Vol. 2, No. 1, Washington, D.C.: TransAfrica Forum (Summer, 1983).

Truth, Sojourner. "I suppose I Am about the Only Colored Woman . . ." Fourth National Woman's Rights Convention, New York City, 1853, and Convention of The American Equal Rights Association, New York City, 1867. Lerner. op. cit., pp. 566–572.

Wade-Gayles, Gloria. "Anatomy of an Error." *Catalyst*. Premiere issue. Atlanta, Georgia: Fulton Public Library, 1986, pp. 50–53.

————. "Black Women Journalists in the South, 1880–1905." Callaloo, Nos. 11, 12, 13, Vol. 4, No. 1–3 (February/October, 1981).

————. *No Crystal Stair: Visions of Race and Sex in Black Women's Fiction*. New York: The Pilgrim Press, 1984.

Walker, Alice. *The Third Life of Grange Copeland*. New York: Harcourt Brace Jovanovich, 1970.

————. *In Love and Trouble*. New York: Harvest Book, Harcourt Brace Jovanovich, 1973.

————. *The Color Purple*. New York: Washington Square Press, Pocket Books, Simon & Schuster, 1982.

————. *In Search of Our Mothers' Gardens*. New York: Harcourt Brace Jovanovich, 1983.

————. "In The Closet of the Soul: A Letter to an African-American Friend." *Ms.* (November 1986), pp. 32–33.

Walker, Margaret. *For My People*. New York: Arno, 1969.

————. *Jubilee*. New York: Bantam, 1981.

Wallace, Michele. *Black Macho and the Myth of the Superwoman*. New York: Warner Books, Inc., 1978.

————. "The Color Purple—'An Amos 'n' Andy' for the '80s." *The Village Voice*, Vol. 31, No. 11 (March 18, 1986).

Washington, Mary Helen. *Black-Eyed Susans: Classic Stories by and about Black Women*. New York: Doubleday, 1975.

————. *Midnight Birds: Contemporary Black Women Writers*. New York: Doubleday, 1980.

Watkins, Mel. "Sexism, Racism and Black Women Writers," The New York *Times* Book Review. (June 15, 1986).

West, Dorothy. *The Living Is Easy.* New York: Arno Press, 1948.

Wilkinson, Roris Y. and Ronald L. Taylor, eds. *The Black Male in America.* Chicago: Nelson-Hall, 1977.

Wilson, Harriette. *Our Nig.* Edited by Henry Louis Gates. New York: Random House, 1984.

Wright, Richard. "Blueprint for Negro Writing." *New Challenge II* (Fall 1937), pp. 53–65.

———. "How Jim Crow Feels." *True Magazine* (November 1946), pp. 25–27, 154–156.

———. *Black Boy: A Record of Childhood and Youth.* New York: Harper & Brothers, 1945.

———. *Native Son.* New York: Harper & Row, 1940.

Wright, Sarah. *This Child's Gonna Live.* New York: Dell, 1969.

INDEX

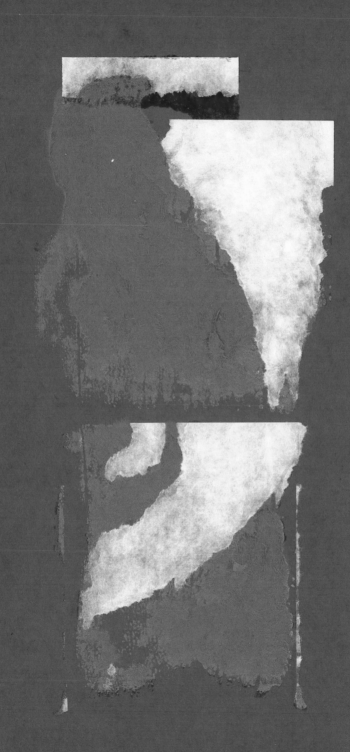